ICONS OF
MEN'S STYLE

ICONS OF MEN'S STYLE

JOSH SIMS

Published in 2011 by Laurence King Publishing Ltd
361–373 City Road
London EC1V 1LR
United Kingdom

Tel: + 44 20 7841 6900
Fax: + 44 20 7841 6910

e-mail: enquiries@laurenceking.com
www.laurenceking.com

A catalogue record for this book is available from the British Library.

ISBN: 978-1-85669-722-4

Design: Rudd Studio
Picture Editors: Christina Borsi and Heather Vickers
Printed in China.

CONTENTS

INTRO.

In the world of popular culture, an icon is typically a person who, through capturing the spirit of the times, or, more accurately, having it imposed on them by the media, comes to represent a certain trait. There are icons of fashion and style, of sexuality, and of masculinity. They are the 'greats' of their time, emulated by many, inspirational to many more, and their iconic status often remains long after they have died. So it may at first seem strange that menswear might also have its enduring icons – and especially that these might be inanimate and not the heroes of Hollywood, among them Fred Astaire and Steve McQueen, whose cinematic roles or personal style made them timeless templates for a way with dress.

While the women's wardrobe has its classics – lasting styles often reinterpreted and frequently updated – there are arguably more of these in the men's wardrobe. In part this is because womenswear is more a product of fashion, which can be defined as frequent change for its own sake. Menswear, on the other hand, is also a product of fashion but this tends to be apparent only in the details, in a ponderous, evolutionary advancement rather than in sweeping statements. Men's styles are variations on a recognizable, well-known theme, rather than a new score altogether. Ever since the English dandy Beau Brummell ushered in a new, sober, fitted restraint in menswear in the early nineteenth century, peacockery has been largely shunned. Conservatism in clothing has been the mark of the gentleman. Consequently, much of the men's wardrobe – key looks, acceptable colours, standard silhouettes – has been largely the same for perhaps a century or more.

This is not to say that these decades have not seen changes. There has been innovation, much of it a product of necessity and utility: items of clothing, accessories and accoutrements that by fast fashion's standards may look old and staid today, but which in their time broke new ground. For all their subsequent and enduring ubiquity, they were once brilliant examples of design in the purest sense – made not for flash but for function. A problem was identifed, then textiles and issues of cut, comfort and cost, wear and use were managed together with the demands of large-scale manufacturing to provide an ideal solution.

Many products met the particular demands of work, sport or the military so successfully that they established new standards and spawned countless imitations. Others were simply the peak of a long, ill-defined process of refinement that made them generic of their type. Almost certainly, any man reading this book has more than a few of them in his wardrobe.

Indeed, in being the first of their kind, or in perfecting the brave, forgotten failures of before, these items have formed what might be called menswear's canon. They created the benchmarks for all subsequent versions of their kind. This is not to say they cannot be improved on; creative and inventive designers have made the most of the latest technologies to devise men's clothing and accessories that are, in some regards, superior to the originals – perhaps in ease of wear, lightness, durability, utility and sometimes quality, if rarely in terms of sheer style.

These benchmark products might also be said to have had luck on their side. In some instances a case can be made for recognizing that a close forerunner or contemporary pushed the same boundaries around the same time, and in similar ways. For some unfathomable reason – maybe a matter of commerce, maybe because many of the companies or organizations behind the products still exist today, or perhaps simply because of the mysterious, fate-like process that culminates in 'cool' – it was the items in this book that captured the imagination.

They continue to do so, suggestive as many of them are of adventure or – in a past seen in nostalgic soft-focus – of times when all men were stylishly dressed, whether they were on their way to the track, about to swab the deck, chop down a tree or simply stroll through the city. These, then, are the icons of menswear and their stories. Some have had their moments in fashion. Others have been co-opted as the uniform of a defining subculture. All of them are hard to beat.

ALAN LADD

1.
OUTERWEAR

THE BLOUSON

OUTERWEAR

Not content with being a thorn in the west's side during the late 2000s, president of Iran Mahmoud Ahmadinejad became an unlikely style leader. The reason was his signature fawn cotton blouson, known to foreign correspondents as the Ahmadine-jacket, which was sufficiently inspirational for Iranian entrepreneurs to order container-loads of copies from Chinese manufacturers for the president's more loyal followers to wear in the bazaars.

Ahmadinejad may not be too keen on the fact that the blouson – neat, simple, casual, comfortable, smarter than a denim jacket, not as loaded with stereotype as a leather one – has also been the choice of powerful men in the west. United States president John F. Kennedy was a fan, though only while sailing; Bill Clinton was snapped in a blouson so often it almost became his trademark garment; George W. Bush liked wearing one to make announcements on the decks of aircraft carriers.

Indeed, the blouson – also known as the windbreaker, golf jacket or Harrington – is almost official attire for US presidents. The United States Air Force supplies one embroidered with the presidential seal to each holder of the office, for wearing on Air Force One. In contrast, there is an everyman quality to the blouson, born of it being the public service utility garment of postal workers and firefighters, police officers, delivery men and parking wardens.

Clearly the blouson's functionality is a large part of its appeal: it is lightweight but showerproof, and easy for all ages to wear. But the jacket became a menswear staple in the second half of the twentieth century through pop culture. It was adopted as part of the 1950s teenage uniform that prefigured preppy style and, 20 years later, by the skinhead and mod movements in the United Kingdom. This was largely thanks to the pioneering London retailer John Simons and his store Ivy Shop, which saw queues to buy blousons; The Clash were fans of the jacket for their Times Square concerts in 1981.

Opposite: James Dean played the archetypal teenager in 1955's *Rebel Without a Cause*. The blouson is worn with a certain insouciance – almost undone, but not quite – allowing that other 1950s youth essential, the T-shirt, to show.

The style itself dates back to 1937 when John and Isaac Miller, garment-factory owners in Manchester in northern England, first started making their G9 blouson under the Baracuta brand name. Like most of its many imitators, it was an unfussy cotton jacket with a stand-up collar, knitted cuffs, raglan sleeves and slanted flap pockets. The G9 came with a distinctive Fraser clan red, green and black tartan lining, the use of which was permitted by Simon Fraser, 24th Lord Lovat. The company also made rainwear (it supplied the macs for the 'demob' outfits for British troops in 1945 and for England's World Cup-winning squad in 1966). But by 1950, when Baracuta began to export to the US, the G9 was stealing all the limelight. When Elvis Presley wore the style in *King Creole* in 1954, and James Dean wore a similar jacket in *Rebel Without a Cause* in the following year, its status as a staple was assured.

Steve McQueen became an adherent, and wore a G9 when he was photographed riding one of his many motorcycles for the cover of *Life* magazine in 1963. And the following year Ryan O'Neal wore the G9 in the smash-hit television series *Peyton Place*. His character's name? Rodney Harrington – hence the jacket's informal moniker. In 1966, even Frank Sinatra wore one, in *Assault on a Queen*. However, it was not a style to be contained by the world of cool. The roomy, showerproof blouson was also practical on the golf course: when Arnold Palmer launched his first golfwear collection in 1970 he collaborated with Baracuta on the jackets.

Left: Steve McQueen on the cover of *Life* magazine in 1963 – the year *The Great Escape* confirmed his status as a global star. McQueen's love of the relaxed blouson seemed to reflect his love of action man hobbies. **Below:** Arnold Palmer helped to make the blouson an essential item of golfwear: wind- and waterproof but easy to move in. **Opposite:** Actor Daniel Craig as James Bond in *Quantum of Solace* (2008), wearing the smarter – though here rather battle-scarred – G4 version of the Baracuta jacket, with a slimmer cut and without ribbed cuffs or hem.

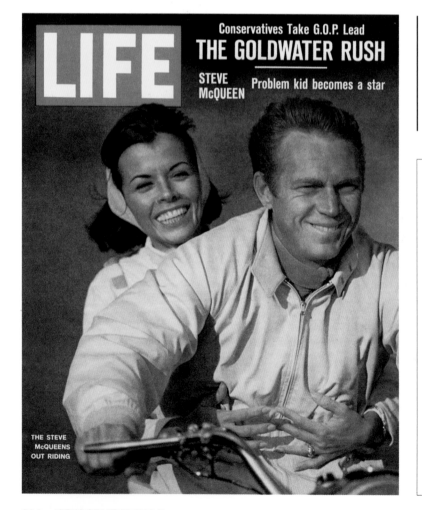

THE WAXED JACKET

OUTERWEAR

The cover is dated 1908 and reads 'John Barbour & Sons – Oilskin Clothing, Factors & Warehousemen – Market Place, South Shields'. It was for the first catalogue produced by the purveyor of tough, all-weather clothing for use chiefly by seamen and dock workers some 14 years after John Barbour, a Scotsman born in 1849, started his dry goods retail business. But it was not until 1980, some 70 years later, that Barbour, still a family company, came to be known internationally and its jackets attained iconic status.

This was the result of a photograph selected for the 1980 catalogue. It showed a good-looking young couple, in the English country uniform of green wellington boots, flat caps and Barbour jackets, walking their Jack Russell terrier across the fields. Although one of John Barbour's sons, Malcolm, had extended the company's sales targets in 1906 to include farmers, the image was still a long way from the brand's grimy, hard-working beginnings. Indeed, it epitomized a new breed of urbanite with pretensions to country living: the country of manor houses and Range Rovers rather than of dawn starts and mucking out. So definitive was the type, named the Sloane Ranger by cultural commentator Peter York, that it both divided opinion – the Sloane was a figure equally of aspiration and approbation – and, in part, defined the decade.

The image also seemed to be in defiance of what until then had been the utility and specialization of Barbour's garments and the signature waxed-cotton fabric from which they were made. Although it was no longer in the biking market, the company had provided some of the first motorcycle clothing in 1911 and launched the acclaimed International jacket, also for bikers, in 1936. It had created the Ursula foul-weather suit for British submariners in the Second World War, named after the U-class submarine of the same name. And it would later be known for its Cowan Commando style worn during the Falkland Islands conflict of 1982. Yet in its 1980 catalogue the jacket was being co-opted for a new country fashion.

BARBOUR'S BEACON

SPECIAL LIGHT-WEIGHT COAT.

We sell the SYLKOIL Beacon Coat in large quantities, it is only 3½ lbs. weight and is made of fine texture cambric, silk finished, non-sticky, double all through, bound with leather, button holes stayed with leather, velvet collar, one inside and two outside pockets. A popular coat for many years with officers of the merchant service, and an ideal coat for

YACHTING

FISHING

DRIVING

BOATING

WALKING

SHOOTING

Post paid
21/-

Never in the way, it stows into a very small space when not in use. Wears well, looks well, and is absolutely weatherproof. Stocked in black only, (yellow in 14 days, 1/- extra).

Left and below: Barbour's heritage lies in making industrial clothing for fishermen and workers in other all-weather trades. But it was the image of the gentleman farmer, created during the 1980s, that relaunched the Barbour jacket as a style item and Sloane staple.

Above: Barbour's graphic identity has changed through the decades but a checked lining has always been a characteristic of its jackets. The tartans might lead some to assume that the Barbour hails from Scotland, rather than north-east England.

Two styles captured the public imagination, and cemented Barbour's shift from being a maker of 'industrial' clothing to one of 'countrywear'. The Bedale, launched in 1980, was a short, lightweight, thornproof style designed by company chairman Dame Margaret Barbour as an equestrian jacket. It had many of what have become trademarks of a Barbour jacket: big, bellows pockets, corduroy collar and brass, ring-pull, two-way zip fastening. The Beaufort was developed two years later as a shooting jacket, based on styles Margaret Barbour had seen on visits to France (hence its Frenchified name), where shooting clothing was driven more by the needs of functionality than the sport's sartorial codes.

The Beaufort was originally available only in sage, which has effectively become a house colour for the Barbour brand. It added to the company's trademarks two hand-warmer pockets, and a full-width, rear pocket for game, lined with nylon so the blood could easily be washed away. Not that its many city-dwelling fans saw much of this. They were more impressed by the fact that the jacket was worn by members of Britain's royal family when they were at Balmoral in Scotland. The Queen gave her Royal Warrant to Barbour in 1982, and the Prince of Wales gave his in 1987.

Inevitably, cheaper copies of Barbours have flooded the market – a backhanded acknowledgment of their classic status – and the popularity of the jackets has moved through cycles that have distanced them from their Sloane beginnings. Today they are respected as much for function as for country fashion.

THE OVERCOAT

OUTERWEAR

A coat created by a Scottish family business that dates back to 1772 may be an unlikely style totem for Teddy boys, mods and skinheads. But in its various guises the Crombie, as it was affectionately called, became as much part of their considered and particular uniforms as certain polo shirts or shoes.

The coat was part of the menswear canon long before the 1950s and 1960s. John Crombie was born into the family weaving business and in 1805 established a woollen mill in Aberdeen with the original idea of selling quality cloths not only to merchants but direct to tailors. This meant there was something of an association with sartorial exactitude long before Crombie first made coats under its own name, in the 1880s. Early in the company's history one breakthrough model was nicknamed the 'Russian coat', largely because it was designed to protect the wearer from what was imagined to be the kind of cold experienced during the harshest Siberian winter.

Another coat, created specifically for the Russian royal family to wear in the country, was the Covert – from the French *couvert*, a shady place or thicket – which had a contrast velvet collar, ticket pocket, poacher's inside pocket and distinctive bands of reinforcing stitching at the cuff and hem, and was made in a smooth, thornproof, fawn or charcoal fabric. It became the template for the classic Crombie overcoat, although Crombie and another British company, Cordings, established in 1839, have disagreed about which of them pioneered the style; Cordings claims that its founder, John Cording, created it as a riding coat as far back as 1877.

The Cordings coat was later selected for the permanent fashion collection in London's Victoria & Albert Museum. But Crombie's business success in the late nineteenth century, notably through exports across Europe, and to America and Russia (where the overcoats became widely popular with the aristocracy), meant that its name was sometimes used incorrectly to describe a certain simple style: a coat made from thick, dense, dark wool, single-breasted (sometimes with a fly front), with narrow lapels and straight cut to just above the knee. Its

Opposite: Salvador Dalí arriving in London in 1955, wearing a double-breasted Chesterfield-style coat, with complementary alligator-skin case, cane and waxed moustache. **Right:** The young Prince of Wales in 1912, later King Edward VIII and, following his abdication in December 1936, Duke of Windsor. **Below:** An example of the classic Covert-style coat, with its characteristic ticket pocket.

reputation has lasted: when the Russian premier Mikhail Gorbachev visited the west to pursue his policy of glasnost he wore a Crombie.

The Crombie's reputation for fending off the big freeze also won it military contracts – a sure stamp of approval. The first was with the Confederate army during the American Civil War (1861–65), when the colour of the cloth from which the coats were made became known as rebel grey. Coats were supplied to the French when Paris was besieged by the Prussian army in 1871; anecdotally at least, one customer ordered a Crombie via a hot-air balloon. The so-called British Warm – double-breasted, with peak lapels and epaulettes, and sometimes belted – was worn by British officers during the First World War.

By the 1930s, however, heated interiors and travel by car meant very heavy fabrics were no longer needed, and lighter-weight versions of the Crombie were developed. The coat became an undisputed part of the male wardrobe, to some extent because it was favoured by the likes of Edward, Prince of Wales, as well as Winston Churchill, Frank Sinatra and United States presidents Dwight D. Eisenhower and John F. Kennedy. Certainly, the fact that it was considered the stuff of officers, gentry and power brokers only reinforced the perception that a Crombie was a coat for the upper classes. This was a perception that style movements from the 1950s onwards subverted by making the coat their own – the Crombie has been the coat of statesman and gangster alike.

Opposite: Gary Cooper with a dapper, peak-lapel overcoat and the up-and-coming Mexican actress Lupe Vélez in 1929, fuelling rumours that the couple were engaged.
Left: Frank Sinatra arrives at London airport in 1956, prepared for the cold. **Below:** US President-elect John F. Kennedy and US President General Dwight D. Eisenhower leave the White House in Washington for Capitol Hill for Kennedy's inauguration ceremony in 1961.

THE DENIM JACKET

OUTERWEAR

When Bing Crosby was refused entry into an upmarket hotel during the 1950s because he was wearing a denim jacket, Levi Strauss & Co. made him a tuxedo – in the same fabric. It was a neat riposte. The jacket had been a staple of the working world for some 70 years, which is why its appearance at a swanky venue might have been unexpected, but this is why its many variations, most of them a take on a simple, waisted, breast-pocket style, have appealed to the outdoorsmen and pioneer workers for whom they were originally created, and to ranch hands and beat intellectuals, heavy metal rockers and artists.

The first denim jacket probably dates to the 1870s and followed hard on the heels of the first denim jeans (early jacket records are unclear because the San Francisco earthquake in 1906 destroyed the archives of many workwear companies). Long defunct names, such as Boss of the Road, Stronghold and Heynemann (which launched in 1851 with its catchily named Can't Bust 'Em brand), made various kinds of work clothes in denim. However, Levi Strauss & Co. introduced the first riveted denim jacket; after all, it owned the patent on the device.

The company made other jackets: sack styles in around 1910 (looser fitting and designed to be worn over bib overalls); blanket-lined (a trend that came and went until it became fashionable again in the 1950s); jackets made of duck, a heavy canvas fabric… But the first to sketch out the archetypal style was the lot 506 'pleat front blouse' of 1905, with stitched pleats that could be unstitched to provide more room for warm layers, a chest pocket and a buckle-back that pulled the jacket into a fitted form. It was so popular that a budget version, the 213, had to be introduced.

With each generation Levi's evolved the style. The 506 may have become a favourite of rocker Eddie Cochran but it had also inspired imitations, like H.D. Lee's 401 jacket of 1925. Levi's 507 jacket, the so-called type 2, introduced in 1953, added an extra pocket but did away with the buckle-back in favour of side-adjusters, deemed at the time to present a cleaner, more modern look.

Opposite: Bing Crosby in full denim attire, including a Levi's 506-style pleated denim blouse (as the early jackets were called). **Right:** Better known for his pipe and cardigan, Crosby was such a fan of denim that when he was refused entry to a hotel because he was wearing it, he returned on another day in a tuxedo he'd had specially tailored in the same fabric. Since then the denim jacket has become almost signature for men such as the pop artist Peter Blake.

Opposite: The Lee Storm Rider jacket, with blanket lining and corduroy collar, first launched in the 1930s.
Above: There were many variants on the idea of the denim jacket in Levi Strauss & Co.'s early days, as this late nineteenth-century advert shows.

This style also had its imitators, such as Wrangler's first jacket, the 11MJ; early examples of this incorporated vents to allow additional freedom of movement.

In 1962 Levi's introduced its preshrunk 557XX. With its two flapped pockets placed higher on the chest and distinctive V-shape seams running from pockets to waistband, it was widely considered to be the classic 'trucker' style (a name conferred on it by fans rather than the company). It was, indeed, favoured by long-distance haulage drivers, even though Levi's targeted the jacket at ranch workers – much as it had its definitive sawtooth Western shirt of 1938. Perhaps the 557 came too late for this market. In the 1930s the line of Dude Ranch clothing, of which it was a part, had been aimed at city dwellers and hinted that the cowboy lifestyle was dying out and moving into the realm of myth. Instead the 557 was picked up by riders of metal steeds and came to symbolize the *Easy Rider* counterculture.

If Levi's defined the jacket used for industrial and general purposes, the Western market had other favourites. In 1933 H.D. Lee introduced its slimline 101J jacket – the companion to its 101 jeans and its first original piece of cowboy clothing. The same year saw the launch of the Storm Rider jacket, essentially a 101J with blanket lining and a corduroy-lined collar, which became the cowboy standard for the next three decades, in fiction as in real life: Kirk Douglas sported one in *Lonely Are the Brave* (1962), as did Paul Newman in *Hud* (1963) and, perhaps most influentially of all – even for men – Marilyn Monroe in *The Misfits* (1961).

THE DUFFLE COAT

OUTERWEAR

It is ironic that the commander of Britain's Eighth Army during the Second World War, who led his Desert Rat troops to victory over Rommel in the sweltering heat of El Alamein in North Africa, should be so closely associated with a heavy, hooded coat designed to tackle the cold of the North Atlantic. Field Marshal Bernard Montgomery's image was defined in part by his distinctive and sometimes shabby wartime dress – his grey, knitted sweater and, most famously, his beret – but was perhaps best captured by his preference for a duffle coat.

For a military design the duffle coat has a somewhat cosy reputation, as the choice of Peruvian bear (and children's storybook character) Paddington, and the uniform of the British nuclear disarmament movement of the late 1950s. But the basis of the style predates the Second World War considerably: 'duffle' comes from the Belgian town of Duffel (now part of Antwerp), where a heavy woollen cloth with a high lanolin content that makes it naturally water-repellent has been woven since the Middle Ages. It was used to make coats for Royal Navy personnel during the First World War, but not in the duffle style.

The duffle coat's characteristic fastenings – large wooden toggles slotted through rope loops – could easily be manipulated with cold hands and were thought to have originated with Belgian peasants who used whatever basic materials were available to them. The coat retained its humble nature. During the Second World War, when what might now be recognized as the duffle coat was manufactured to Britain's Ministry of War specifications as a Royal Navy general issue item, coats were rarely assigned to any one serviceman. Rather, one was picked up and worn by whoever needed it, officer and rating alike. The style's loose fit made it workable for just about every size and shape. Few classic movies of naval warfare – the likes of *The Cruel Sea* (1953) for instance – are free of the duffle coat. David Bowie later wore one in *The Man Who Fell to Earth* (1976).

It was Field Marshal Montgomery who popularized a coat that was originally designed for seafarers, and was considered rather shabby and shapeless by the officer classes. A twist had the same coat, cheap and abundant through its availablity as army surplus, adopted by protesters on the first Campaign for Nuclear Disarmament march, from London to Aldermaston in 1958.

The duffle's transition to civilian wear came about only because so many coats were surplus to requirement after the war. The Ministry of Defence contacted M. & F. Morris Industrial Clothing, a specialist supplier of overalls and chain-mail gloves, for assistance in getting them to market. To make the coats more appealing to a public tired of war and anything associated with it, in 1951 the company's head, Harold Morris, conceived a brand name: Gloverall.

Demand for Gloverall coats – affordable, durable and very warm – was such that when the surplus supplied ran out the company began to manufacture them, albeit in a more streamlined, fashion-friendly version styled by Morris's father, a master tailor. The bucket hood was scaled down, flap pockets were added, a new double-faced woollen cloth in navy and tan was used (rather than the Royal Navy's undyed dun colour), the wooden toggles were replaced with horn ones and the rope loops with leather. The benchmark style was called the 512 and by 1955 it was being exported. The French film-maker Jean Cocteau, playing on the coat's everyman, democratic leanings, was photographed wearing one, not just among café society but also on grand occasions. Actor James Stewart was a fan. John F. Kennedy wore a 512 for sailing during winter.

For all its new glamour – albeit of a homely kind – the duffle coat never lost sight of its hardy roots. In 1979 the members of the British Transglobe Expedition wore them, as did members of the British Winter Olympic Team in 1980 as part of their official uniform. Belgian though its origins may be, the duffle coat has now come to be regarded as quintessentially English.

Opposite: David Bowie, an extraterrestrial in a duffle coat in *The Man Who Fell to Earth* (1976). The musician re-created the image in pop art form for the cover of his album *Low* the following year. It is a long way from the Second World War, when duffle coats kept sailors alive.

THE FISHTAIL PARKA

OUTERWEAR

The 1950s fishtail parka might be considered one of the first 'flexible clothing' systems. With various elements that built up into an increasingly cosseting garment it could be worn in all weathers and conditions. To a loose and light, sturdy cotton outer shell could be added a thick, alpaca-wool pile, button-in liner, then a fur-trimmed hood. Each 'fin' of the fishtail was designed to be tied around the legs to create a more fully insulated, closed environment – and safer, more efficient aerodynamics for paratroopers.

The United States Army had tried to develop such a system during the Second World War, for general cold-weather issue. The OD-7 was a hooded coat plus a liner, made from pile at the start of 1945 and fibreglass in 1947. But neither was successful and after the details had been finessed the M-48 or M-1948 (after the year of its introduction) was issued. This was essentially a top-spec version of the initial concept, complete with a pocket on the arm – an idea borrowed from the MA-1 flight jacket (see page 36).

But it was the M-51, or M-1951, introduced in June 1951 during the Korean War (1950–53), that saw the parka style more widely distributed. The first winter campaign had been disastrous in part because of the lack of cold-weather clothing, and this had provided the incentive both to keep costs down and to supply more troops with parkas. The M-51 was mass-produced and cheaper than its predecessors: the pile lining and extras like the sleeve pocket were removed and the fur trim was replaced with a synthetic one. If the liner was removed the shell gave some protection during Korea's monsoon summers.

The M-51 initially came with epaulettes and an attached lightweight, fold-down hood, with button fixtures that allowed a heavier hood to be worn over it. There was also an attempt to retain the feel of the M-48 by using similar heavy fabrics. But these were slow to dry. A second generation of the M-51 was created in lighter, faster-drying materials, with a cotton and wool lining, that gave added mobility without too much loss of warmth. It also came in olive green rather than olive drab, the standard army shade during and since the Second World War.

Opposite: Rock Hudson in *Ice Station Zebra* (1968), the all-time most parka-friendly film, trumping even the mod story *Quadrophenia* from 1979 (illustrated on page 35).

The M-51, arguably the definitive version of the parka. Introduced as a less expensive version of its predecessor, it was rushed into production to supply US troops fighting through Korea's extremely cold winters – the official design spec cited 'a parka designed to be worn over other clothing at mean monthly temperatures below +14° Fahrenheit (-10° Celsius)'. Unfortunately, fabric supply problems meant most of the parkas that were made did not reach the soldiers until the conflict was almost over. The coats that were intended to be issued to front-line troops often ended up with soldiers in the rear. This led to an overhaul of the army's quartermaster system. The M-51 came in olive green, not olive drab, in part because the top brass thought the flood of army surplus items in the latter, worn by labourers after the Second World War, had devalued the shade.

The M-51 was produced in the United States for only five years, and then in Allied-occupied Germany, where it was made by German companies for another three. Aside from contract orders for foreign militaries, notably those of Canada and the United Kingdom, the style was dormant until 1965 when its next evolution, the M-1965 or ECW (Extreme Cold Weather) parka, was designed. Its shell was made of a cotton/nylon blend, treated for additional waterproofing, and it had a single detachable hood. It remained in service until 1987 when it began to be phased out.

But it was the M-51 that gave the parka its moment in fashion. In the United Kingdom during the late 1950s and 1960s the mod movement and cheap army surplus supplies of the now redundant garment came together and the M-51 was deemed ideal for keeping rain and dirt off a sharp tonic suit while riding a Vespa scooter. Indeed, that the parka is as much part of mod iconography as the movement's preferred mode of transport was assured in 1973 when The Who featured it on the cover of their concept album *Quadrophenia* – this was realized as a film in 1979 and sparked a second, more populist fashion life for the parka, complete with pin badges and patches.

THE FLIGHT JACKET

OUTERWEAR

Opposite: The MA-1 jacket is one of the many military clothing items devised by the anonymous designers and fabric technology experts of the testing labs at the US Army's Natick Laboratories in Natick, Massachusetts, and the USAF's Aero Medical Laboratory in Dayton, Ohio. Until the 1970s, when globalization opened up the market, the US Department of Defense contracted these specialist items to a small group of manufacturers – among them New York-based Superior Togs Corporation, Rolen Sportswear and Dobbs Industries – who regularly subcontracted to each other to get the huge orders filled. **Below:** An example of the blood chit, written on the lining of a flight jacket; in several languages, it gave guarantees of reward to anyone who assisted a downed pilot to return safely to base.

The jackets created specifically for the United States military in the years after the Second World War were paragons of functionality and so, perhaps inevitably, have also found a life in civilian service. Foremost among these is the MA-1, a jacket that, for its comfort, ease-of-use and distinctive style, from the 1970s came to be beloved not only by skinheads but also by nightclub bouncers and other security staff, before it also took on the role of a promotional gift, complete with embroidery celebrating a corporate event or band tour on its back.

A nylon flight jacket, the MA-1 was issued to all United States Air Force and United States Navy pilots in around 1950, as a replacement for the B-15. Introduced in the late 1940s this was similar in style to the MA-1 except for its mouton fur collar. Indeed, each jacket evolved from its predecessor in response to the changing needs of servicemen or the introduction of new equipment: the B-15's collar interfered with new helmets issued for use in jet aircraft. The light, windproof nylon B-15 was similarly a development of the B-10, a thick, cotton version introduced in 1943, and itself a replacement for the classic leather flying jackets favoured by United States pilots.

Certain characteristics of the original MA-1 are visible in the B-15 it replaced: sleeve pocket; chest tabs, used to secure radio wires between cockpit and helmet; and chest webbing – a clip for the oxygen mask while taxiing. But by 1960 the B version of the MA-1 had seen the removal of both tabs and webbing – radio and oxygen supply was by then integrated into the helmet. Further revisions were introduced in 1963: for flight crews, the sage-green lining was replaced with one in bright orange – known as Indian or rescue orange – and the jacket was reversible. Downed pilots wore their jackets bright side out to be more visible to search and rescue parties. This is arguably the most iconic of all versions of the MA-1.

Over the years of its development, other sibling jackets for the US Air Force (and, before 1948, its predecessor, the US Army Air Force) were widely appreciated by civilians. The L-2B, an MA-1 lookalike in summer-weight nylon, introduced soon after the end of the war, was the first jacket to have an orange lining and, until the mid-1960s, also had epaulettes. The N-2B flight jacket, issued in the late 1950s, was a sage-coloured version of the navy-blue N-2A and effectively a cold-weather MA-1, complete with fur-lined hood.

King of the nylon jacket manufacturers was clothing entrepreneur Samuel Gelber's Alpha Industries, which is still in business thanks to its foresight in developing a civilian market – for example, by issuing the MA-1 in colours other than the standard air force sage green or army olive green. Jackets made for the civilian market are also identified by three lines on the labelling. This was before many of Alpha's fellow manufacturers were forced to close down by a combination of international competition and a decline in government contracts, which diminished sharply after the boom times of the Korean and Vietnam wars. By then, however, the MA-1 was well on its way to becoming a classic.

Above: Jack Lemmon in *It Should Happen To You* (1954).
His shabby appearance belies the mac's early royal
endorsement: in 1825 the Duke of York wore a crimson
silk-lined blue cape made from Macintosh fabric on parade
and sparked a trend among guardsmen. In 1843, Macintosh
amalgamated his business with Thomas Hancock of
Manchester, who patented a rubber treatment process he
named vulcanization, after Vulcan, the Roman god of fire –
some eight weeks before the American Charles Goodyear,
of tyre fame, applied for the patent. Goodyear claimed he
had discovered the process in 1839 but was sadly unable to
convince his sibling business partners of its potential.

THE MAC

OUTERWEAR

That the generic term for the raincoat is mac – an Americanism spread through post-Second World War Hollywood, and arguably now superseded in general parlance by the computers from Apple – is a testament to the originality of the idea pursued by one Charles Macintosh.

A chemist born in Glasgow in 1766, the son of a textile dye manufacturer, and a man with a fondness for experimentation, Macintosh inherited the family business on his father's death in 1823. Soon afterwards he discovered that coal-tar naphtha could dissolve India rubber, then an expensive novelty material with limited industrial use that included tubing for medical devices. The world's first waterproof fabric was created when he realized this rubber solution could be shaped into sheets that could be laminated on to cloth. The early fabric was not ideal. Macintosh first used wool to create a material that was both warm and waterproof, but the resulting coat proved almost unbearably heavy to wear, and natural oils in the wool rapidly degraded the rubber. Other combinations tended to turn brittle over time, or the rubber coating melted in hot weather. The first truly successful mac was some years away.

The breakthrough came in 1843, 13 years after Macintosh had amalgamated his business with a Manchester one run by Thomas Hancock, when Hancock patented a rubber treatment process he named vulcanization, after Vulcan, the Roman god of fire. This created a lighter, more hard-wearing and chemical-resistant substance that could be combined with fabric to make a lighter, more flexible and more comfortable garment without sacrificing the coat's all-important waterproof qualities. It also made the resulting material easier to dye and work with, which led to the close-fitting, narrow-shouldered styles for which it was first used, and the later looser, raglan-sleeve style for which the mac is better known. A further construction process – smearing the seams with the rubber solution and taping them – meant water could not penetrate the outer shell of the coat. Older macs tended to develop a characteristic smell that, in time, was masked by adding perfumes to the rubber. It would take

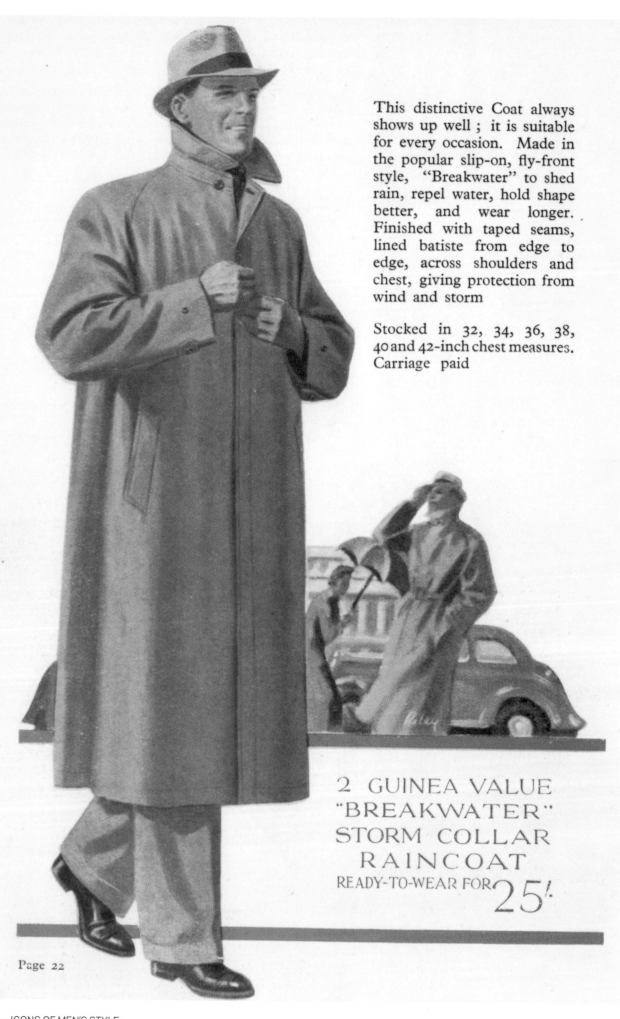

This distinctive Coat always shows up well ; it is suitable for every occasion. Made in the popular slip-on, fly-front style, "Breakwater" to shed rain, repel water, hold shape better, and wear longer. Finished with taped seams, lined batiste from edge to edge, across shoulders and chest, giving protection from wind and storm

Stocked in 32, 34, 36, 38, 40 and 42-inch chest measures. Carriage paid

2 GUINEA VALUE "BREAKWATER" STORM COLLAR RAINCOAT
READY-TO-WEAR FOR 25/-

Page 22

science another 150 years or so to develop fabrics that overcame the mac's last remaining problem: without ventilation (and even with strategically placed breathing holes) it could become stiflingly hot to wear; some doctors spoke of wearers blighted by 'rubber sickness'.

Nevertheless, the mac soon became an established part of the male wardrobe – although dress codes of the late nineteenth and early twentieth centuries meant it was rarely seen in the city. Together with tweed jackets, it was worn only in a rural setting, a dress etiquette that reflected the fact that it was regarded as being purely functional rather than fashionable.

Macintosh and Hancock found themselves with a ready market among more prosperous workers. And the mac's utility was soon recognized by those who travelled by horse, be they coachmen or more well-to-do horse riders. In fact, the Charles Macintosh India Rubber Company, as it was known, suffered its first and only major downturn in business with the advent of the railways and public transport systems that everyone could afford.

Perhaps this made the mac a romantic as much as a practical item – a totem of the British climate and the sartorial struggle of living stylishly with it. 'There is a wild garment that still carries nobly the name of a wild Highland clan,' G.K. Chesterton, writer and creator of the 'Father Brown' detective series, wrote. 'I like to think of all the Macintoshes, in their macintoshes, descending on some doomed Lowland village, their wet waterproofs flashing in the sun or moon...'.

Early macs tended to develop a distinctive and not attractive smell, with the result that a Manchester company, Mandelburg's, offered what it called its FFO (Free From Odour) Mac. The smell did not stop the style becoming a staple of formal dressing: 'And the banker never wears a mac / In the pouring rain / Very strange,' as The Beatles' 'Penny Lane' (1967) noted.

THE BIKER JACKET

OUTERWEAR

Few movie characters have created an icon from their clothing with quite the lasting impact of Johnny in *The Wild One* (1953). Played by Marlon Brando, he is the disaffected youth who, when asked what he is rebelling against, bluntly replies: 'What have you got?' He is also the leader of a biker gang, at a time when such gangs epitomized the outsider threat to society to the extent that many high schools banned their jacket style. This is the point of the joke in *Back to the Future Part II* (1989), in which Marty time-travels to 1955 and, asked to dress to be less conspicuous, buys, like Johnny, a Perfecto jacket.

The Perfecto more than any other garment suggested a kind of anarchy, a reputation rock stars have capitalized on ever since. Johnny Ramone, leader of The Ramones, enforced wearing one as part of the New York band's image. James Dean, the archetypal role model for living fast and dying young, was rarely without his. Its manufacturer, Schott, was not slow to miss a trick. When the machismo suggested by the biker jacket gave way to the hippy counterculture of the 1960s, the company created a fringed leather waistcoat and jacket. But before and since, the bad boy image has ruled.

Irving Schott, the son of Russian immigrants, founded Schott Bros in 1913 to make coats, and was a pioneer from the outset – he is believed to be the first garment-maker to put a zip (manufactured by Talon) in a casual jacket. But his major contribution to menswear would be made in 1928, when a Long Island Harley-Davidson distributor called Beck Industries contacted him and asked him to create a tough, zip-up leather jacket to protect motorcyclists against the weather and unfortunate falls. Beck got what they asked for. It retailed for $5.50 and was called the Perfecto, after Irving's chosen brand of signature cigar.

The original style was distinctive. Made of horse hide, it had a belted front, zip-up sleeve cuffs, hidden collar snaps, several pockets (a D-pocket with a vertical rather than horizontal opening, a change pocket, and a side pocket strategically positioned to make access easier during riding) and epaulettes with studs. But it was two later styles, of the 1940s and 1950s – both slimmer with two side

Opposite: Andy Warhol wears the biker jacket in characteristically quirky style – over a double-breasted suit jacket. Below: The 613 or One-Star version of the Perfecto, dropped in 1963 when retailers complained that the stars were always being stolen.

pockets, no D-pocket, an angled breast pocket and a stud to allow a fur collar to be attached – that would capture the public imagination. And slightly scare it.

They were the 618 and, as worn by Brando's Johnny, the 613 or One Star, named after the star emblem on each epaulette which distinguished it from other biker jackets including ones from Trojan, Buco and, by now, those of Harley-Davidson itself. The stars were dropped in the late 1960s when retailers complained that customers kept stealing them. There have been a few further cosmetic changes. The mitre belt (so called because of its mitred corners) has gone, the lower back panel has changed shape, the zips are two-way and the jackets are only occasionally made from horse hide. Otherwise, the Perfecto is much the same as it was over half a century ago. And just as tough.

Below right: Douglas Colvin, aka Dee Dee Ramone, bassist and lead songwriter for the American punk rock band The Ramones. Their jackets (it was Johnny Ramone's diktat that every band member must wear one), pudding-bowl haircuts and ripped jeans came to epitomize the look of the New York punk scene of the 1970s. In later years Dee Dee Ramone would reject the style: 'It made me feel like a phony standing there in a leather jacket and torn jeans. Four middle-aged men trying to be teenage juvenile delinquents.'

Above: The original juvenile delinquent – Johnny Strabler, played by Marlon Brando in *The Wild One* (1953), the first film to examine outlaw-biker violence in the United States.

THE PEA COAT

OUTERWEAR

With its thick, 32-ounce (900-gram) Kersey wool, double-breasted fastening, extra-tall collar with throat latch, broad lapels and warming, tan corduroy-lined pockets, few coats are as cosseting as the pea coat. Smart though it may be, it is also an ideal garment for fending off the bitter cold at sea – which is why it has been a standard part of the United States Navy uniform since about 1881.

The definitive Naval Clothing Factory pea coat was not introduced until the late 1940s, when it lost the longer line and flap pockets of models issued before the First World War, and gained wider, flatter lapels and one of its most distinctive characteristics today: six large, black, shiny, Bakelite buttons with a fouled-anchor stamp (an anchor wrapped in rope), rather than the crest of 13 stars featured on earlier versions. Although the stars represented the 13 states of America that signed the country's Declaration of Independence in 1776, the pea coat originated in the British Royal Navy. It is derived from the double-breasted, heavy wool reefer jacket worn by midshipmen (also known as reefers), whose duties included climbing the rigging and unfurling the sails – a process known as reefing.

The reefer jacket's essential style may have come to be regarded as typically naval over time, but it was one of the first pieces of standard-issue clothing issued to all services. It was introduced as part of the Royal Navy's 1857 overhaul of dress regulations for all crew members; until then they provided their own clothing (often known as slop) and no consistency was imposed. The officer class had been expected to abide by regulations laid down a century previously. (In the 1940s the heavy pea coat ceased to be standard issue for US Navy officers – who adopted either a more formal version with epaulettes and brass buttons, or a bridgecoat – and was provided only for ratings.)

Like the pea coat that evolved from it, the reefer jacket was highly functional: it was double-breasted to provide additional warmth against cold and wind, and to protect the body against the rubbing of the rigging ropes. The buttons were set to one side (even though one row became decorative as a result), which

Opposite: A classic pea coat from Alpha Industries, contract manufacturers of many military clothing items including the MA-1. **Below:** Steve McQueen and Richard Attenborough in *The Sand Pebbles* (1966).

made it less likely that they would get caught on the ropes. The jacket was cut short to allow ease of movement. It was coloured indigo navy, to hide dirt and also because at a time when there were no colourfast dyes it was the shade most resistant to being faded by sunlight and repeated drenchings by rain and by seawater.

The US Navy pea coats were issued in what was known as midnight or dark navy-blue – barely a shade from black. From 1980, black Melton wool was used. This was just one of the changes that diminished the navy-issue pea coat's quality during the postwar decades, as pressure on military budgets mounted. Others included the elimination of the corduroy pocket lining and cuff-stitching detail in 1967, and replacing the Bakelite buttons with pewter ones in the mid-1970s.

The cloth historically used for pea coats is believed by some to have given the style, variations of which became standardized throughout European navies, its familiar name: pea may well be a corruption of *pij*, a coarse wool cloth woven in the Netherlands during the eighteenth century and used for a typical worker's jacket called a *pijjakker*. Alternatively, the name is simply a misspelling of P-jacket, from pilot's jacket, named for the mariner who guides a ship through congested or dangerous waters.

Opposite: James Cagney wearing an early, cropped pea coat in *The Frisco Kid* (1935).

THE BOMBER JACKET

OUTERWEAR

When Frank Sinatra sought to give his character in *Von Ryan's Express* (1965) a tough-guy image, and Bob Crane required a distinctive piece of military clothing for his role as Colonel Hogan in the United States television series *Hogan's Heroes* (1965–71), their costume departments turned to the A2 pilot's jacket, and sparked a renewed appreciation of it in the process. The same would happen after the release of the film *Pearl Harbor* (2001).

Such is the appeal of this leather zip-up style (known as the bomber jacket even though its use was not restricted to bomber crews) that its pattern, or subtle variations thereof, has come to represent the archetypal flyer's jacket. This is some achievement for a garment designed in 1930, and introduced the following year for the United States Army Air Corps as a replacement for the button-up, knitted-collar A1 model that had been in service for just four years. The A2 was standard issue until 1943, after which it was gradually replaced by cloth jackets.

As with many military clothing contracts, the variety of manufacturers, civilian and specialist, that produced the A2 – among them Cooper Sportswear, the Poughkeepsie Leather Coat Co., Aero Leather, Spiewak & Sons and the Cable Raincoat Co. – saw the introduction of subtle variations in the design. These were of a kind that now excites avid collectors drawn to vintage pieces, not only for the jackets themselves but also for the blank canvas that their one-piece backs provided for budding flyer-artists. If the front of a bomber was the place for nose art – illustrations that blended sex and death, the crew's successful raids counted next to Alberto Vargas-style images of a leggy pin-up after whom the aircraft might be named – the rear of a flyer's jacket was an ideal spot for recording his tours of duty.

Three squadrons – the so-called Flying Tigers of the 1st American Volunteer Group, American pilots who controversially fought with the Chinese air force against the Japanese from 1941 to 1942 – painted a blood chit or escape flag in the space. This comprised instructions in Chinese that any downed

Opposite: Frank Sinatra wearing an A2 jacket as Colonel Joseph Ryan in *Von Ryan's Express* (1965). It was not an original, but was made for him by the film production company's costume department. **Right:** The A2 was so popular with pilots that when it was discontinued in 1943 a number of small manufacturers sprang up to supply servicemen who could no longer get one. The jackets were held in such high regard that, while they were officially only ever available to airmen, Generals Patton and MacArthur also wore them. Wartime publicity shots of James Stewart and Glenn Miller – both of whom saw active service – often had them wearing A2s. Pilots who served in the Korean War (1950–53) continued to wear a model of jacket that had ceased to be official attire almost a decade earlier.

airman should be afforded assistance and protection. It became a distinctive characteristic of the costumes worn by John Wayne and others in *Flying Tigers* (1942), which was passingly based on the squadrons' exploits.

The left sleeve of an A2 typically bore the emblem of the US Army Air Force, while the right was a site for proudly worn squadron patches that were added and removed as a pilot moved between bases (or – a quirk of navy pilots – simply added, one next to another).

Materials varied from issue to issue. Tanned horse hide was the norm, but goatskin and steer hide were also used, with the colour varying between seal (dark brown) and russet (medium brown). But the bare, essential design created a leather jacket that was durable and practical – worn fitted, as it was, it provided essential warmth for aircrews, at least during all but winter operations – and also smart. As on a button-down shirt, the collar was fastened to the body of the jacket with snaps; unlike the A1, the A2 had epaulettes; and, behind the front flap pockets, hand-warmer pockets were popular designs for the civilian market but considered unmilitary as wearers might walk with their hands in them. Until 1939, when cost prohibited it, the jacket came with a silk lining. This was replaced with a cotton lining – for all flyers except the fighter aces of the 56th and 479th Fighter Groups, who, when their fifth kill was confirmed, were entitled to a red satin lining.

In 1988 the US Air Force reissued a goatskin version of the A2 (complete with hand-warmer pockets). Unlike the original A2, it was not available to all airmen who had passed through basic training, but only to those who had completed mission qualifications. Consequently it was all the more prized. Sadly, regulations did not permit recipients to paint the backs of their jackets.

Left: Regis Toomey, in a button-fastening A1-style jacket, with Anita Page in *Soldiers of the Storm* (1933).

Above: Gregory Peck in costume for *Twelve O'Clock High* (1949), an early post-Second World War film about the US Army's Eighth Air Force bomber crews and their daylight raids over Nazi Germany. In real life, when the 351st Bomb Group's plane was shot down over Eggese in Germany in 1943, the Nazis used the airmen's A2 jackets – emblazoned with Murder Incorporated – to 'prove' that the Allies were deliberately bombing the civilian population. Controversial inscriptions or emblems on the jackets of US Army Air Force flyers were consequently proscribed.

THE FIELD JACKET

OUTERWEAR

It is difficult to know whether protesters against the Vietnam War dressed in the M-1965 (M-65) field jacket out of a sense of irony because to do so was to reappropriate a symbol of militarism as one of peace, or because army surplus stores made the jacket affordable, or, indeed, because many of the protestors were ex-servicemen.

What perhaps united all wearers of the M-65, both in and outside the army, was its highly practical style, which makes it arguably the most widely copied military garment and certainly the one that has been most worn in civilian/commercial life. Like the motorcycle jacket, the M-65 has a certain outsider status. Small wonder it has been repeatedly chosen by costume designers – most famously for Robert De Niro in *Taxi Driver* (1976) – or, for that matter, by Osama bin Laden.

The M-65 was a jacket stripped down to its most functional elements: long enough to offer protection, short enough to allow for movement; a nylon/cotton sateen fabric that was wind resistant and almost indestructible; four large flap pockets; a hood hidden in the collar; a nylon quilted liner; tighteners at waist and cuffs to keep in body heat; and, ominously, a triangular attachment inside each of the cuffs to which could be attached gloves designed to further protect the jacket's wearer on a nuclear battlefield.

Reaching this apotheosis of design – subtle variations of which are worn by many armed forces today – took more than two decades. Its first incarnation came in 1943, when the M-1943 (M-43) field jacket was introduced to replace the 1941 standard issue one, then designated not the M-1941 but the Parson's Jacket, after its designer Major General J.K. Parsons. This was a neat, waist-length, almost sporty, zip-up cotton jacket with a button-up fly, flannel lining and a couple of slash pockets (later given buttons). Based on a civilian jacket, it had style but lacked many of the practical benefits of the M-43; notably, it was either too warm or too light, depending on conditions, it lacked pocket space and the light, dun colour was deemed to make its wearers rather too conspicuous for comfort.

In 1942 the Office of the Quartermaster General – the United States Army department that was concerned with the design and supply of equipment – began tackling this issue by developing its first products according to the uniform ensemble layering principle (which was applied most successfully with the parka): various garments could be combined to provide suitable attire for differing combat conditions.

The final design of the M-1943 saw the jacket as an olive drab, cotton-lined sateen shell with four characteristic pockets, a button-up fly front and button-on hood, worn with a pile faux-fur liner in winter or over a cropped M-1944 Ike jacket in more temperate locations. The M-43 was tested in severe conditions: it was worn in January 1944 by the US Army 3rd Division in action around Anzio, Italy, where one of the war's bloodiest battles took place. It passed the tests, although delays and priority manufacturing of other uniform parts meant it did not see widespread distribution until the end of the year. In 1948, when the United States Air Force was established, it created its own version of the M-43, without epaulettes and with a large, crescent-shaped collar.

Further tweaks to the design after the war moved it closer to the M-65: the M-1950 brought a button-in liner; the M-1951, which did not actually come into service until late 1953, introduced snaps for the pockets and a zip to replace the button closure, so that wearers could crawl on their fronts without their jackets snagging on obstructions. Finally, after more than ten years of service, the field jacket was again updated as the M-65. The chief advance was the use of a tougher mixed fabric and, for some forces, camouflage prints. These may have given the garment a more military bearing; without them it remains a classic example of fuss-free functionality.

Below: Field jackets were worn not only by veterans after the Vietnam War – through which the style entered the clothing mainstream – but also, as a result of army surplus, by protesters against the conflict. Scrawled with graffiti, the jackets became sites of personal expression. But the design almost never made it off the drawing board: some Department of Defense parties initially favoured a short woollen jacket like the Ike, or the British army's standard battledress tunic on which it was based. **Opposite:** Robert de Niro as Travis Bickle in *Taxi Driver* (1976). The field jacket also made appearances on Al Pacino in *Serpico* (1973) and on Sylvester Stallone as John Rambo in *First Blood* (1982).

THE TRENCH COAT

OUTERWEAR

When the trench coat became an optional item of clothing in the British army during the First World War only officers were allowed to wear it. Such class associations have long been lost and the coat, and its variations, is an everyman alternative to the classic macintosh, even if distinctive details of its military heritage remain: the epaulettes that secured rank insignia or anything on a strap; the D-ring, at the front and rear, on to which ammunition pouches and other supplies were hooked; and the storm flap at the shoulder, now an extra means of funnelling rain away from the body, and originally devised to provide cushioning against the kick of a rifle butt. Other details add up to make the trench one of the most weatherproof coats ever devised: the throat latch, wrist straps and the rain shield, which works like the storm flap but across the back.

The trench coat may have come to be the uniform of Chandler-esque private eyes of the 1940s – think Robert Mitchum in *Out of the Past* (1947) or *Foreign Intrigue* (1956) – and is famously associated with Humphrey Bogart's Rick Blaine in *Casablanca* (1942). But its story begins in nineteenth-century England with two pioneers in fabric innovation: John Emery and Thomas Burberry. The former owned a menswear shop on London's Regent Street and in 1853 developed the first waterproof wool, which he patented and launched under the brand name Aquascutum (Latin for water shield). He supplied capes, field coats and a forerunner of the trench coat to troops of all ranks during the Crimean War (1853-56). Later his company cornered the market for supplying the movie industry: stars wore the Aquascutum Kingsway trench coat on screen and off.

Thomas Burberry owned an outfitter's shop in Basingstoke, southern England, which was popular with local hunters, fishermen, horse riders and cyclists. He created gabardine, made from chemically coated, long staple cotton yarns woven so tightly into a distinctive diagonal twill that, while air could pass through it, the fabric stood up to rough treatment and fended off rain. It was consequently colloquially known as duck. It was not initially used for clothing. Its first test came when explorer Roald Amundsen bought tents made of gabardine

Opposite: Michael Caine as Jack Carter in *Get Carter* (1971). Below: An early advertisement for the Burberry trench coat. Below right: Robert Mitchum, whose roles in *Out of the Past* (1947) and *Foreign Intrigue* (1956) helped to boost the trench coat's popularity.

for his 1911 race to the South Pole. He gave the fabric what amounted to a hero's endorsement: 'Burberry gabardine is extraordinarily light and strong and keeps the wind out completely.' Ernest Shackleton was entirely kitted out in Burberry gabardine for his 1914–16 Antarctic expedition. The company's first raincoat – before the trench – became the standard, named the Burberry when it proved impossible to trademark its initial name, the Slip-On.

The clearest move towards the definitive trench-coat style came in 1899 with the Boer War in South Africa, when many British officers unofficially adopted Burberry weatherproofs; the company became one of the official outfitters to the British army in 1901. Its first military-specification coat was the Tielocken, so called because it tied at the front with a strap and buckle so securely the wearer was locked into it; this belt became a distinguishing characteristic of the trench coat. Some half a million Tielocken were supplied during the First World War. Aquascutum's version reached even more officers through its Aquascutum Service Kit – a box that contained everything the well-dressed man needed to take to war, bar the weaponry.

Initially anonymous, the Burberry trench-style garment was nicknamed the trenchwarm by officers who valued its cosy properties, especially the detachable sheepskin liner. It was so successful the *New York Times* of 29 August 1917 reported 'Trench Coats in Demand...' and added, 'it is expected that a coat very similar to this, if not this particular coat, will be included in the men's regular equipment when the American forces finally arrive at the front'. Not just the officers' equipment, it might be noted. It was only a small step for the trenchwarm to be officially named the trench coat. Few officers were ready to give up their coats when the war ended – and the style entered civilian life and sartorial history.

Left: The characteristic details of Burberry's and other gabardine trench coats. First World War-era versions had detachable sheepskin liners, which officers behind the front line often wore like dressing gowns. Gabardine was inspired by traditional clothes worn by English shepherds and named after the garment worn by Caliban in Shakespeare's *The Tempest*.

Above: Humphrey Bogart helped to make the trench coat a movie star through his roles as detectives Sam Spade and Philip Marlowe, and, most famously, in *Casablanca* (1942).

2.
TROUSERS

KHAKIS / JEANS / CARGO PANTS /
BERMUDA SHORTS

KHAKIS

TROUSERS

Traditionally, flat-fronted khaki trousers, or, more simply, khakis, are a standard casual alternative to jeans, and their strongest associations are with the United States Army during the Second World War and with the preppy style of the 1950s. Their roots, however, can be traced back a further century.

The story begins in 1845, in India. In one version, in an early attempt at camouflage, British soldiers deliberately discoloured their white uniforms, which made them conspicuous targets, with mud, the distinctive local dust, coffee and even curry; khaki means dust-coloured in Urdu. In another, Sir Harry Lumsden, commander of the forces in the Punjab, replaced his regulation trousers with lighter, looser pyjama bottoms to cope with the heat. He had them dyed with tea leaves and later realized that they were also useful as camouflage.

In 1848 the British army recognized the military advantages of a colour that blended into the environment and officially adopted khaki for the warm-weather uniforms worn by its troops in India and in subsequent late nineteenth-century campaigns in South Africa, Sudan and Afghanistan. These were originally made in China, ostensibly to save on transport costs, but demand was such that by the 1850s khaki fabric was woven within the British Empire; John Haller, a weaver from Europe, introduced the first hand looms to the Indian region of Mangalore and the invention of khaki dye is usually attributed to him. As a consequence, khaki became a standard colour for the uniforms of armed forces in many countries.

It was not until 1898, during the Spanish-American War, that American troops adopted uniforms of a similar cut and colour. Chino, which has come to describe a more generic casual cotton trouser (khakis, by definition, are chinos in a specific dun colour), is a corruption of the Spanish word for Chinese. The style's general utilitarian use was soon pursued commercially: Levi's, for example, launched its first khakis in 1906 under the Sunset label.

Opposite: Phil Silvers as Master Sergeant Ernest G. Bilko, with his right-hand men Corporal Rocco Barbella and Corporal Steve Henshaw. Each week on *The Phil Silvers Show*, which ran from 1955 to 1959, the khaki-clad trio tried and failed to swindle their superiors.

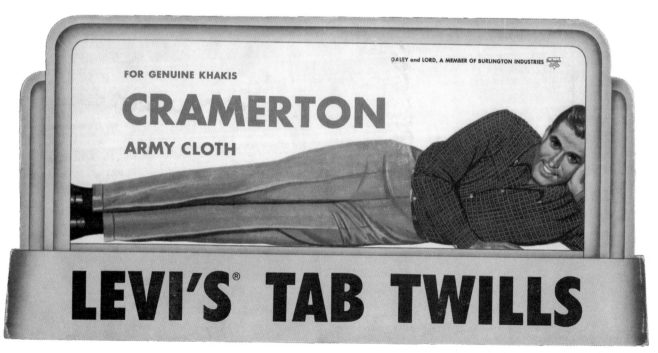

New Campus Classic!

LEVI'S®
CINCHBACKS
SANFORIZED

NO PLEATS
NATURAL SLIM LINES

Above: Khakis were one item in the military uniform that US veterans of the Second World War wanted to wear in civilian life, and soon became a staple of any young man's preppy wardrobe. **Right:** Sunset was one of the early sub-brands that was launched by Levi Strauss & Co. to produce non-denim clothing.

Khakis were officially adopted by the United States Navy in 1912 as part of the uniform worn by naval aviators. They were worn by submarine crews from 1931. Ten years later, in 1941, during the Second World War, khaki trousers made from a tough, twill cloth called Cramerton, created by weavers Galey & Lord, were approved as part of senior officers' uniforms during on-station duties; at the end of the same year permission to wear them during spells of 'liberty' was granted. Two further regulation styles were issued in 1942 and 1945. The khakis worn by British servicemen were a darker shade (known as British khaki) than the US versions, and GIs referred to them as suntans.

After the war, assisted by the huge quantities of cheap army surplus clothing that were available, khakis soon found a role in civilian life. They aged well, were functional, comfortable and hard-wearing, and their style and neutral colour allowed them to cross over. In a big way. They were symbolic of adventure – pioneering aviator Charles Lindbergh and action-man novelist Ernest Hemingway favoured the style – but it was nevertheless their adoption by Hollywood that ensured khakis became a menswear staple. Men's men James Stewart, Humphrey Bogart, Gary Cooper, Clark Gable and James Cagney, and later John F. Kennedy, Steve McQueen and bohemian literary types such as Gore Vidal, were all snapped wearing them.

JEANS

TROUSERS

Not even Levi's are sure why their 501 jeans are so called. Until around 1890 the original version, which featured a cinched back and buttons for braces, was designated XX on its leather patch, meaning the highest quality denim had been used. From 1886 the jeans featured the brand's famed two-horse logo, which depicted the animals trying, and failing, to pull a pair of Levi's jeans apart – a handy depiction of the product's durability for anyone who couldn't speak English. But although the style's new description – 'lot 501 patent riveted waist overalls' – appeared a decade shy of the new century, quite why it did so was lost on 18 April 1906 when Levi Strauss & Co.'s headquarters, and the company's archives, were destroyed in the earthquake that devastated much of San Francisco. Certainly 5 had been designated for any top-tier garment.

Jeans, possibly the single most iconic garment of the twentieth century, were the brainchild of Jacob Davis, a Latvian immigrant and tailor who serviced workers on the fledgling American railroad. He was asked to make working trousers that would not fall apart, and hit upon the idea of riveting the stress points on what was then a jeans-style garment made of white cotton duck. He needed a partner to realize his ambitions, and in 1873 he and Levi Strauss, a Bavarian immigrant and successful dry-goods wholesaler, patented the rivet using Strauss's money. The result was the first pair of jeans – then better known as waist overalls – made of 9-ounce (255-gram) denim from the Amoskeag Mill in Manchester, New Hampshire, and sewn in San Francisco.

Jeans proved to be the ideal, superstrong garment for miners and cowboys, railwaymen and lumbermen; and some 70 years later 501 jeans were symbolic, somehow simultaneously, of generational unity and individual rebellion. Jeans were the garment not only of workers, but also of bikers, rockers and peaceniks and, ultimately, everyman and -woman.

Reaching this stage was an evolutionary process of details. The original 501 jeans had only one rear pocket, on the right, featuring the Arcuate – an arc of stitching (machine-sewed by eye until 1947). This was perhaps originally used

Opposite: Paul Newman, whose many Westerns included *The Left-Handed Gun* (1958), *Hud* (1962), *Hombre* (1966) and *Butch Cassidy and the Sundance Kid* (1969). **Below:** Levi's jeans were first worn not by cowboys but miners: one of the oldest pairs in the company's archive was discovered in a mine. In 1920 Levi's received a letter of complaint from a miner called Homer Campbell stating that the jeans he had worn for six days a week for three years had not held up as well as the pair he had worn for 30 years previously. On closer examination the jeans were fine. Only the patches he had added for extra protection had shredded.

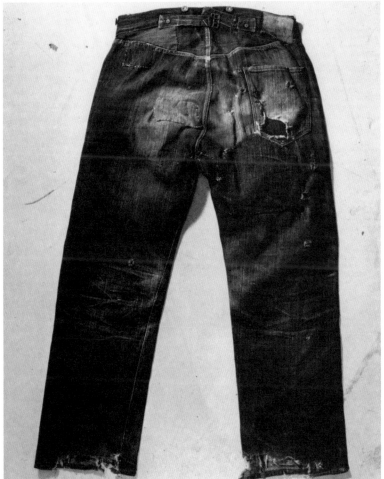

to hold a pocket lining in place, but worked more effectively as an early form of branding that was sufficiently successful to be copied by Levi's competition. In 1901 a second rear pocket – referred to as the fifth pocket (a small one for watches was among the other four) – was added. Belt loops came in 1922, probably because braces were falling out of fashion. By the 1920s the denim was supplied by Cone Mills in Greensboro, North Carolina, which, by the end of the decade, had developed a 10-ounce (280-gram) red-selvage denim called O1 that was used exclusively for the 501.

In 1936 a red tab devised solely to distinguish the style from copyists was sewn into the back pocket edge; the capitalized lettering went lower case in 1971. And in 1937, after cowboys complained that the rear-pocket rivets scratched their saddles and housewives that it ruined the furniture, the pockets were sewn over the rivets. This was also the year when buttons for braces died out (although Levis Strauss continued to provide 'press on' buttons for those who wanted to avoid newfangled belts).

The Second World War brought the last key changes, and the style has remained largely the same since then. Because of a shortage of raw materials, the Arcuate was temporarily replaced with a painted version and the crotch rivet was removed. (The rear-pocket rivets went in 1966 when technology allowed equally tough stitching.) Come 1947 the slim-line, streamlined 501 style recognizable today was born. And was finally ready to go national – until then the jeans had been available only through retailers in Western states. Soon they would go global.

Get the real thing!

LEVI'S®

AMERICA'S FINEST JEANS • Since 1850

Opposite: Lee has long been Levi's main rival. It made a speciality of supplying jeans for urban and industrial workers rather than ranch-hands, but despite this its most famous model is the 101 Cowboy style. The 131 cinch-backs are also characteristic of Lee's contribution to the hard-working life: the blank leather patch on the rear pocket was designed to be branded with the name of the owner of the jeans.

Lee
Highest Quality
WORK CLOTHES

It's **Lee** 6 to 1

THE H. D. LEE COMPANY

Kansas City, Mo. • South Bend, Ind. • Trenton, N. J.
Minneapolis, Minn. • San Francisco, Calif. • Salina, Kansas

In a nationwide survey* among thousands of men doing all types of work, the question was asked . . . "What brand of overalls do you prefer?" Lee Jelt Denim Overalls led the next brand by a margin of 6 to 1.

Why is Lee the choice of commonsense, money-wise workingmen? Because they *know* bedrock work clothes value! They know Lee's exclu-

sive fabrics wear longer and wash better. They know Lee "Tailored Sizes" mean perfect fit, lasting comfort and better appearance.

Buy Lee Work Clothes . . . at leading stores coast-to-coast.

THERE'S A LEE FOR EVERY JOB!
JELT DENIM OVERALLS • UNION-ALLS • MATCHED
SHIRTS AND PANTS • DUNGAREES • COWBOY PANTS

Survey made by a prominent publishing company.

WORLD'S LARGEST MANUFACTURERS OF UNION-MADE WORK CLOTHES

CARGO PANTS

TROUSERS

People first carried small pouches tied to their waists in the medieval period, and interior pockets in clothing were introduced in the late eighteenth century. But it was another two centuries, the latter half of which saw the steady build-up of professional armies, before the utility of putting extra pockets on the trousers of service personnel on active duty was recognized. Before combat or cargo pants, today as much a standard in fashion as in fighting, image was more important than usefulness – the overspill of an ethos that saw military dress as being all bold colours and brass buttons: pomp and pageantry rather than practicality.

Jump forward to the 1930s and the European programmes of rearmament. These included the growing mechanization of armies, most notably in ammunition-hungry machine guns and anti-tank rifles. It soon became apparent to the British War Office that a distinction needed to be made between battledress worn in action and service dress, worn off duty and less particular in its requirements beyond the need for smart presentation.

Trials of a new battledress – initially known as Field Service Dress (FSD) – took place in the early part of the decade. Safari-style jackets were considered but their length hindered movement. The final design, arrived at in 1937 and tested on a small scale throughout that year, was little different to the service dress adopted in 1902, except that it had dark buttons that did not require polishing and bag-type pockets.

The FSD was introduced in 1938 – the eve of the Second World War – at first in denim, which was found to be too light and insufficiently warm, and then in heavy khaki serge. Trousers were cut in a looser shape that used fabric more economically (a major concern for a potential war economy) and took its cue from contemporary designs for skiers, which allowed better ease of movement.

Not everyone approved of the new rational design. But at the time it was arguably the most advanced in the world. Every detail of the new look had been considered, down to what should be carried in each of the new pockets: one to the rear, for personal effects; one pleated pocket front right, for field dressing; and one large flap pocket (with hidden button) on the left thigh, in which to store maps. Tabs at the ankles made gathering the material easier before adding gaiters, which themselves replaced expensive high leather boots.

With the exception of minor revisions from late 1942 – to save money the P40 austerity design saw belt loops and ankle tabs removed, and a simple button-through map-pocket flap added – the 1937 battledress (BD) design became the standard for British infantry from the outbreak of the war until 1960. The first combat trousers had been created; other Commonwealth nations introduced their versions of the design throughout the war, as did the United States with what it called its European Theatre of Operations (ETO) uniform. The design was so successful that when the German forces captured large stockpiles after the fall of France in 1940 the trousers were issued to U-boat crews.

Yet more pockets were added to the trousers in 1942; a specialist uniform for United States paratroopers saw another large 'cargo' pocket on their lightweight cotton twill trousers. Even then, it seems that Department of Defense designers and soldiers in the field were somewhat at odds: paratroopers often added a further cargo pocket themselves, the only servicemen who were generally allowed to make personal modifications to their uniforms.

Opposite: During the Second World War distinctive pockets on the trousers characterized the uniform worn by US paratroopers – who often added an additional pocket, making them the only servicemen generally permitted to make alterations to their official uniform. **Below:** The British Field Service Dress of 1938, here in the standard wool serge.

BERMUDA SHORTS

TROUSERS

Opposite: Strolling through New York City in the late 1950s; in the heat of summer Bermuda shorts were a practical, if somehow alternative, choice. Below: Tailors were inspired to design jackets to be worn with Bermuda shorts. Bottom: The one-time national dress for men in Bermuda, complete with tasselled loafers, club tie and knee-length socks.

**PRESENTING OUR EXCLUSIVE KILT JACKET...
DESIGNED TO BE WORN WITH BERMUDA SHORTS**

With the tremendous and ever growing popularity of Bermuda shorts there has arisen the need for a shorter sport jacket to wear with them. Our answer to this problem is an interesting, good-looking modification of the authentic Highland day jacket which is worn with kilts. It offers trim lines, casual styling and just the right balance of length to complement Bermuda shorts.

We believe it will be one of the most attractive, practical and widely accepted style innovations that we have ever introduced.

550 Two-button model Kilt jacket with back vent and fine detailing... in a natural color Brooksweave, finished to look like linen. Brooks sizes 39 to 46 and 48, regulars, longs $45

551 Our well-tailored pleated or plain front Bermuda shorts of a lightweight, comfortable medium or oxford grey flannel. In even sizes, 30 to 42 $18.50

Shorts may not rank highly in the menswear-style stakes. They are all too suggestive of the uniforms of Scouts and private schoolboys, and it's all the better to keep knee holes, those signs of an adventurous life, to a minimum. Arguably, in an age before childrenswear comprised scaled-down versions of 'adultwear', they helped children to think and behave like children. They were acceptable for grown men only on the sports field – plus fours were worn for golf from the 1890s, while the first tennis shorts were not seen until 1932 (on Bunny Austin in the United States men's championships in New York).

Except, that is, for men who lived on the island and British Overseas Territory of Bermuda, from whence come Bermuda shorts, the progenitor of smart shorts. They have been worn here since the 1930s to a strict dress code – pleated and 7.5 centimetres (3 inches) above the knee, together with blazer, regimental tie, tasselled brown or black loafers and knee-length 'Bermuda hose' – as work and even evening attire. 'The short-pant is a terrible fashion choice,' as Winston Churchill had it. 'Unless it is from Bermuda.'

Bermudas are the grandfather of shorts worn today for summer weekends, on vacation and even, in some cultures, to the office. They were part of the Bermudan national dress until 2007, when their association with the island's colonial past and the British armed forces saw their status downgraded. Indeed, the shorts originated with these same armed forces. Bermuda became a military outpost for the Royal Navy in 1816, when the island became its North Atlantic headquarters. Anecdotally, one Nathaniel Coxon ran a tea shop that became a hot spot for the navy. In its crowded interior the heat, always unbearable on the island, grew until the staff complained that their uniform of blazer and khaki trousers was uncomfortable. Coxon's cooling, money-saving solution? Each pair of trousers was cut off just above the knee. All it took then was for Rear-Admiral Mason Berridge, a tea-shop regular, to see the style – he is said to have judged it to be 'a bit of old Oxford and a bit of the Khyber Pass' – and adopt it for his officers. He added the knee-length socks to smarten up the overall look.

The shorts spread throughout the British armed forces, worn by troops serving in tropical climates who had long shortened their standard-issue trousers when permitted to do so. Which came first – Coxon's practicality or that of the British squaddie – remains unclear. What is clear is that in Bermuda the Royal Navy uniform reflected back on island life; Bermudans found their own distinctive style. Ironically perhaps, men typically wear shorts in every hue except khaki, which is worn only by schoolboys.

In making long, smart shorts an acceptable part of the male wardrobe – sufficiently masculine for Ernest Hemingway to become a big fan – Bermudans harked back to menswear history. By the early nineteenth century men had been wearing what were better known as breeches for over two centuries; made of wool for winter and cotton or linen for summer, they fitted the thighs and were buckled or buttoned just below the knee. For the Elizabethan man the selection was wide: trunk hose (very short breeches), slops (baggy breeches) or galligaskin (very baggy breeches), not to mention French, Venetian and *plunderhosen* styles. Gentlemen slashed their breeches to reveal a brightly coloured underlayer. On some, additional strips of different-coloured fabric fully covered this lining; with a nod to the name-calling that might result were a man to wear such shorts today, the breeches were said to be 'pansied'. It was not until around 1825 that trousers came into favour, and breeches were subsequently worn only on very formal occasions.

3.
SHOES

THE SANDAL / THE DESERT BOOT /
THE BASKETBALL SHOE / THE WORK
SHOE / THE WORK BOOT / THE LOAFER /
THE DRIVING SHOE / THE BROGUE /
THE DECK SHOE

Above and opposite: Out in nature with a growing family might be the typical image of sandal wearers, but the back-to-basics appeal of the Birkenstock sandal belies the pioneering engineering, design and understanding of physiology that went into its creation.

THE SANDAL

SHOES

Flower power may have been waning in the early 1970s, but a hippy style of dress lingered in fashion. If society's sartorial rule-book could be epitomized by the three-piece, pinstriped city suit, freedom from its strictures was perhaps best represented by the sandal – the shoe of caravanning couples, nature lovers and fans of an alternative lifestyle. It was not a shoe for a man's man. Until, maybe, 1973, which saw the launch of the Arizona, suggestive as the name was of the great outdoors, of cowboys and frontiersmen even. But a name can be misleading.

The Arizona was a two-strap sandal from a then little-known German company called Birkenstock. Everything about it was unmanly, given the hirsute, barrel-chested concept of masculinity at the time. It was, like much in the 1970s, brown. It had two big buckles. And it was orthopaedically correct, with a footbed shaped like a footprint in wet sand that supported the foot in the correct way shoemakers had long ignored, moulding itself to the shape of the foot over time. The footbed was designed to improve the sandal-wearer's posture, and was even right-on: it was made of a mixture of latex milk from the bark of the caoutchouc tree and cork, which absorbed moisture and had an antibacterial effect. Some people considered the sandals ugly. Certainly, they were unconventional. Yet men took to them. Indeed, not since the uniform of Roman centurions had a sandal been so macho. The award-winning Arizona came to define the masculine face of this type of footwear, winning the sandals the affectionate nickname of 'Birkies'.

Birkenstock had long been a progressive family company, as concerned with improving the functionality of its shoes through engineering as with their style. In 1969, the year of Woodstock, it created the first malleable thermal cork for orthopaedic use. In 1973, the year the Arizona was launched, it developed the first electromechanical moulding machine, which enabled footbeds to be made in different lengths and widths on one adjustable mould. Its products were designed with the same attention to ergonomics as might be afforded a car or cellphone; indeed, its next key product, a thong sandal launched in 1982, took three years to develop and led to eight patents being registered. The company was market leader in the development and use of environmentally friendly glue, the additional cost of which was offset by using less of it. At the end of the millennium it produced the first superlightweight EVA clog, as well as a sandal collection that used no glue at all.

Remarkably, the company has been creating specialist footbeds since 1896, when it was run by Konrad Birkenstock; his ancestor, Johann Adam, had first set up in business as 'vassal and shoemaker' in 1774 in Bad Honnef, 48 kilometres (30 miles) south of Bonn. Konrad's ideas were radical: he spent 16 years travelling around Germany and Austria, lecturing with other master shoemakers and explaining his footbed ideas with a view to creating a network of licences. The company got its break in 1915, during the First World War, when the orthopaedic workshop of the Frankfurt Friedrichsheim Hospital hired it to custom-make shoes for wounded soldiers; the hospital director agreed to sponsor its designs. Ten years later the 'blue footbed' became Birkenstock's first international commercial product. Its greatest hit would not be for another 50 years or so.

THE DESERT BOOT

SHOES

The Clarks desert boot is one of the most versatile of men's footwear styles. It can take the formal edge off a suit, as Savile Row couturier Hardy Amies explored during the 1960s. It looks sharp with a deconstructed jacket, and is a dressier alternative to sneakers when worn with jeans. The boots even look good teamed with baggy khaki shorts, as they originally were: after all, they have 'legendary qualities in hot climates', as the company's advertisements declared in the 1950s.

Perhaps these qualities are what caught the eye of Nathan Clark of the C. & J. Clark shoemaking family, based in Somerset, England. During the Second World War, when he was serving in Burma with a West African brigade, he spotted what he described as 'crêpe-soled rough suede boots' on the feet of off-duty Eighth Army officers who had previously been fighting in Egypt. They had been made for the officers in the Old Bazaar in Cairo, where a more rough-hewn version was worn by traders. Clark was under the impression that, in turn, the style was derived from the boots of South African soldiers, which were based on the *veldschoen* (shoes for the open country) worn by Dutch Voortrekkers.

In 1949, after his return to Somerset, Clark asked pattern-cutter Bill Tuxhill to re-create the supercomfortable, streamlined construction: a two-piece upper, back stiffener and crêpe sole on a wide, round-toe last. Many people at the company were convinced the boot would never sell but Clark thought otherwise; its pioneering sole was the first comfortable alternative to leather. Desert boots were a big hit in the United States, where they were first appreciated as part of the preppy look, as a consequence of both an editorial in a 1950 edition of *Esquire* and the company's imaginative launch of the style at the Chicago Shoe Fair: Clark re-created a desert oasis, complete with belly dancers who presented the boot on a silk pillow.

Although it was a British-made product, the desert boot was not launched in Europe for another 15 years, when it was so successful that in Italy it came to be regarded as quintessentially English, and in France any desert boot, original or copy, became known as *les Clarks*. The style has been a favourite of style and cultural icons over the decades – Steve McQueen (in 1963's *The Great Escape*), Bob Dylan and The Beatles were fans – and is a recurring stalwart of many style movements. The desert boot was the choice of the mods of the 1960s and 1970s, hiphop crews of the 1980s (customized with a marker pen), house music fans in the 1990s (comfortable enough for dancing until dawn) and its popularity has continued to the Brit Pop era of the 1990s, and beyond.

The desert boot has come in many forms: made in Harris tweed, patent leather, tartan checks, in recycled shirting fabrics, in the red, white and blue of the Union Jack… But the classic remains suede, as supplied from the start by the Charles F. Stead & Co. tannery in Leeds, northern England.

Clarks has a knack for discovering classics. In 1964 Lance Clark launched the Wallabee, another soft shoe whose design seems to defy easy categorization. And in 1974 the Desert Trek – a variant of the desert boot, with a lower cut and a centre seam over the upper – was introduced as a response to the oil crisis, when more people took to the streets to walk to work.

Opposite and below: First seen on the feet of traders in Cairo's Old Bazaar, desert boots were an unofficial part of British army uniform for soldiers serving in North Africa during the Second World War. It took Nathan Clark's commercial version to make them part of the uniform for beatniks and mods.

Clarks days
are back again.

ORIGINAL
DESERT BOOT Clarks

THE BASKET-BALL SHOE

SHOES

Opposite and below: From blue suede shoes to white canvas pumps: Elvis Presley thrusts his pelvis in a pair of Jack Purcells, one of the key styles from the Converse stable. However, none of them has topped the Chuck Taylor basketball model, an early version of which is shown below.

How the Converse All Star originated is a story that belongs to more innocent times. Back in 1921 an established basketball player, Charles, or 'Chuck', Taylor, walked into Converse's Chicago offices looking for a job. These were the days before celebrity ruled the world and the company didn't sign him up as the new face of their product – they hired him as a salesman. Taylor duly sold the brand's basketball boots, and in the 1930s Converse decided to add his name to a product.

Taylor's boss was Marquis Mills Converse, the manager of a footwear company who in 1908 had decided to go it alone and launch his own business. The Converse Rubber Shoe Company, based in Malden, Massachusetts, had soon established a firm reputation with its gent's rubber-soled shoes. It broke into the tennis shoe market in 1915 and launched the Converse All Star basketball shoe two years later. It was a ground-breaking style, but it was the Taylor version that resulted in the company claiming an icon.

The shoe had all the design enhancements Taylor suggested, most notably the patch to protect the ankle. But it was his sales efforts that ensured what came to be known as Chuck Taylors were the official shoes for physical training in the United States Army during the Second World War. His salesmanship also led to the first Converse Basketball Clinic being established to improve the basketball skills of college students across the United States – and persuaded coaches and local sporting goods stores to switch to Converse shoes. By 1949 the All Star was the official footwear for every player in the National Basketball League, the forerunner of the National Basketball Association.

Taylor was a salesman and frontman for the basketball shoe for some 48 years, until he died in 1969. More importantly he also oversaw the simple canvas All Star boot, or hi-top, as it became part of American folklore. Only available in black until 1947, when an all-white version was introduced, the boot became as much part of the teenage and collegiate uniform as denim and checked flannel shirts, and was a choice of the era's rockabilly subculture. This was largely down to clever marketing: each year the company produced the *Converse Yearbook*, which celebrated the highlights of the basketball year and included high school athletics. It came complete with illustrations by Charles Kerin, whose work, along with that of Norman Rockwell, created the archetypal imagery of the 1950s American Dream.

By the 1960s Converse dominated the athletics footwear market – in 1966 it even decided to introduce seven colour options for the boot. However, its time at the top did not last. Rival companies were launched throughout the 1970s; Converse failed to innovate and was eclipsed by more technically advanced designs from the likes of Nike and Adidas.

Nevertheless, Chuck Taylors – also affectionately referred to as Chuckies, Connies and Cons – have continued to retain the loyalty of many fans and, from the late 1970s onwards, have been well worn by key, typically music-led, subcultures, including American punk rock, grunge (Nirvana's Kurt Cobain rarely wore any other footwear), G-funk – the bass-heavy variety of American West Coast rap/hiphop – and, at the turn of the twenty-first century, the goth-esque style of hardcore punk/EMO. With such a strong following outside sports, it's small wonder that the Converse All Star can claim to be the best-selling athletics shoe of all time.

THE WORK SHOE

SHOES

Rather than being named prosaically after a stockroom number, the Dr Martens 1460 boot is so called because the first one came off the production line at the R. Griggs shoemakers in Wollaston, Northamptonshire, on 1 April 1960 (1/4/60). The eight-holed, cherry-red boot was distinctive from the outset, as was the shoe version, the 1461, launched the following year. But, unexpectedly perhaps, given the clumpiness of this footwear, the 1460 was about comfort rather than appearance, and once the pains of breaking the boots in had been overcome they were extremely easy to wear, especially compared with other work footwear of the time.

'It's a fact! The working man has never before been offered a really comfortable boot,' an advertisement for Dr Martens declared in 1960. '"Hard work – Hard boots" had to be accepted. The revolutionary Dr Martens Air Cushioned soles puts an end to this foot-breaking torture... a most pleasant experience for the much abused foot.'

Although the famed Airwair sole is now considered to be a characteristically British product it was invented by a German during the Second World War. Dr Klaus Maertens, a 25-year-old who was home from the front, was convalescing after a skiing accident in 1943 and had the idea of making an air-filled material for soles that would help his painful foot. This came to fruition when he teamed up with Dr Herbert Funck, a mechanical engineer. The two men bought up the disused rubber to be found abandoned at Luftwaffe airfields and devised a method for heat-sealing, rather than stitching, the sole on to a shoe's upper, which created airtight compartments (which later proved useful for inventive drug-smugglers).

The DM, as their footwear came to be known, had inauspicious beginnings: it was sold as being ideal for older ladies, for gardening. It was not until 1960 that the Griggs shoe business acquired exclusive manufacturing rights, made design changes that would define the DM's characteristic look for boots and shoes alike – bulbous shape, ribbed welt and yellow welt-stitching – and decided

Opposite: Punk has been just one of the sartorial subcultures to adopt the Dr Martens boot as part of its uniform – a look and an attitude that was a long way from the conformity of the police officers or postmen who were once issued with the same brand of footwear.

on an anglicized Dr Martens as its name. 'Dr Funck's' was rejected as a brand name on the grounds that it was potentially offensive.

The comfortableness of the DM ensured it was a staple of public service uniforms – from post office and railway workers to London Underground staff and police officers (who were often instructed to cover the yellow stitching with black ink) – for some decades. But, almost uniquely, its look also captured the imagination of every youth subculture from the 1960s to the 1990s, until the advent of the sneaker as a fashion item, which saw tougher times for the footwear and for the Griggs company.

DMs were worn (and customized) by punks, goths, grungies, hard mods and, most notably, skinheads – both the original working-class ska fanatics and the later nationalistic variety who would come to taint all skinheads. 'Skins' preferred them in brown, with black polish smeared into the creases to 'antique' them, often oversized, with laces passed through the Airwair heel tag and tied around the leg; trousers were worn short enough for this to be seen. They were worn by The Clash, Slade, Madness and The Who's Pete Townshend.

DMs became something of the everyman shoe or boot. Football hooligans found the steel toecaps useful, to the extent that during the 1970s police made fans abandon their DMs outside football grounds. At the other end of the spectrum, teenage girls discovered, through DMs, that they did not have to dress 'prettily'.

Opposite: As Pete Townshend sang of skinheads in The Who song 'Uniforms': 'Wear your braces round your seat / Doctor Martens on your feet / Keep your barnet very neat / For credibility on the street.' Here, police search mods. It would not be long before they were confiscating football hooligans' DMs.

THE WORK BOOT

SHOES

Just as Timberland's 'yellow boot' became a standout flagship style for the company, so the Irish Setter work boot, with what would become its distinctive white sole and its russet-reddish leather upper that mimicked the coat of the dog after which it was named, came to be an emblem for its manufacturer, Red Wing. A template for work boots, this 1930s style also built on a kind of Americana – a blue-collar chic, arguably originating with Levi's 501 jeans, that appreciated the authenticity and hard-wearing qualities of products built for a purpose: for mining, chopping wood, stoking a steam engine, driving big trucks. Engineer boots with their wrap-over buckle, which date back to around 1933 but have long since been co-opted by bikers, have the same appeal.

The Red Wing company was started in 1905 by Charles Beckman, a German immigrant who named it after a town of just 16,000 people, set in the bluffs of the Mississippi River in Minnesota. The town was itself named after the Dakota tribe's chief, Red Wing, the first of whose predecessors was known – appropriately for a boot company – as Walking Buffalo.

The territory was ideal for selling hard-wearing boots. It comprised huge forests, farmlands and iron mines, all subject to extremes of weather: searing heat in summer and temperatures as low as -30°C (-21°F) in the winter. With heavy industry in the region expanding, Red Wing boots found a ready market, most notably for its Brown Chief farmer's model of 1919. The predecessors of the Irish Setter were launched in the 1920s as the company's first 'outing boots', which were specifically designed for outdoor leisure pursuits, in particular, hunting, fishing and boating. War provided the company with an even more buoyant market: it supplied the United States Army with its No.16 boot in the First World War, and again in the Second World War, when it was available in 239 sizes and widths to ensure comfort on long marches.

But it wasn't until the 1950s and early 1960s – the classic era of Americana to which retro trends most frequently return – that the Irish Setter, seemingly designed to look just so with jeans, became a popular leisure boot across the United States. Perhaps nothing could drive this point home more succinctly than the fact that the advertising images of the time were drawn by Norman Rockwell, whose hard-working, hard-playing red-cheeked characters, straight from Main Street, helped to define the era in the popular imagination.

Red Wing boots might play an even greater role in street culture's history if a costume designer hadn't given way to an actor. Harrison Ford was slated to wear a pair when he played Indiana Jones in Steven Spielberg's *Raiders* film franchise. But Ford suggested an alternative: the boots made by another United States bootmaker, Alden, that he had worn when he was a carpenter. This boot may now be known as the Indy but it cannot claim the rugged heritage of the Red Wing.

Opposite: The much-imitated Red Wing classic work boot; its distinctive russet colour gave it its name – the Irish Setter. The style, with its characteristic white sole, had undergone a long evolution. Earlier models had a plain sole with a distinct heel piece, more akin to the styles Red Wing had developed for other specialist activities, including logging and driving locomotives. **Below:** An early Red Wing advert for its Farmer's Shoe model, driving home how the company positioned itself as a provider of footwear to manual workers. Much later its blue collar reputation was sealed by being worn by Jack Nicholson in *One Flew Over the Cuckoo's Nest* (1975).

THE HOME OF
BLACK and BROWN CHIEF
THE FARMER'S SHOE
RED WING SHOE COMPANY

RED WING BOOTS

BEST

UNDER THE "SON"

THE LOAFER

SHOES

The origins of the modern loafer are as much in accident as in intent. American shoe manufacturers were looking for a style that would be definitively their own, rather than effectively an import from the famed English shoemaking towns in Northamptonshire. It came during the 1930s when New Hampshire-based Spaulding marketed a soft, slip-on style of shoe it called the loafer, with everything the name implied of comfort and leisure.

Around the same time, in 1936, an employee of G.H. Bass, also an East Coast manufacturer, based in Wilton, Maine, brought a hand-sewn, moccasin-type shoe back to the company after a trip around Norway. The style was traditional to the indigenous Sami people and Scandinavian fishermen, who wore the shoes when they were not at sea, and was also associated with Native Americans, who wore rough-hewn deerskin shoes without stiff soles to aid movement – silent movement at that. These were so comfortable that they were worn by early traders – and by the end of the eighteenth century settlers in America were sending the shoes to Europe. One story has it that fishermen in Norway adopted them when Norwegian explorers returned from North America, creating a circular exchange.

Inspired by its employee's find, Bass added a thick sole in order to make the style sturdier, dressier and suitable for the United States market, as well as what would become the design's most celebrated aspect: a vamp saddle or strap with a cut-out, diamond-patterned slot. It called the style the Weejun, a corruption of Norwegian.

The slot was intended to be a purely decorative detail. But when American college students began to wear the style – comfortable and smart, but sufficiently casual to avoid being corporate – during the period after the Second World War that saw the birth of the teenager, they slid a coin into the slot, hence the style's nickname: the 'penny loafer'. One company, Kerrybrooke, even produced a shoe, the Teenright Smoothie, complete with a good luck coin. Such was the loafer's almost overnight popularity that the University of Carolina's newspaper, *The*

Opposite and below: Michael Jackson in characteristic dance mode: his loafers gave his feet freedom to move, while his choice of white socks is said to have been in homage to the white spats worn by Fred Astaire. Jackson could afford to put more than a nickel in the penny slot.

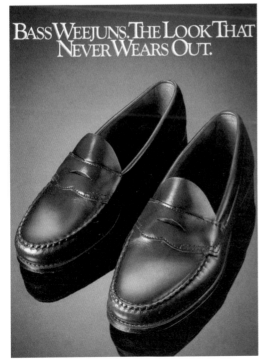

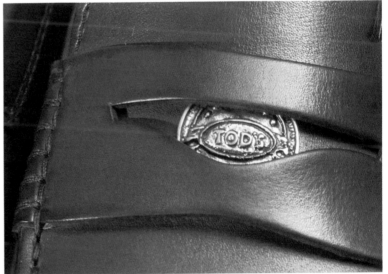

Daily Tar Heel, ran an article that asked 'What are Bass Weejuns?', and declared wearers of the shoes were 'with it'. Almost inevitably, James Dean, embodiment of the 1950s teenage archetype, made loafers part of his uniform of denims and white T-shirt. Elvis Presley wore a white pair in *Jailhouse Rock* (1957).

The pennies were not the only flourish that added distinction to an otherwise streamlined style. In 1952 – supposedly at the request of actor Paul Lukas, star of 1938's *The Lady Vanishes* and 1943's *Watch on the Rhine* – US shoemakers Alden (also an East Coast company, from Massachusetts) created the tassel loafer. For them the tassel, in effect a lace that passed through the shoe's upper and ended in a knot of leather, was not only a debonair touch; it suggested the shoe fitted so well without laces that none were required. When Brooks Brothers decided to carry the style from 1957, the loafer's place in the preppy wardrobe was assured. Other decorations followed. US brand Sebago, for example, introduced the beef-roll – a thick tube of stitched leather at both ends of the vamp saddle. Kiltie fringes were also popular, as was the Venetian style with no vamp saddle or decoration. Gucci's lighter-weight, status-symbol style – beloved of the likes of John Wayne and Clark Gable – replaced both slot and tassel with a snaffle bit.

With its informality, ease of wear and a certain insouciance, the loafer is the quintessentially American shoe for men, popular in Europe only among subcultures such as mods and skinheads. By the 1960s increasingly it was worn not only at weekends but also to the office, even as John F. Kennedy was popularizing the wearing of Weejuns without socks. It was with socks – thick white ones – ankle-skimming trousers and a sci-fi-style red leather jacket created by costume designer Deborah Landis that Michael Jackson chose to wear his patent-leather version some two decades later, in 1984, in the video for his 'Thriller' single. Loafers subsequently became a signature style for the singer.

Opposite and below: Loafers epitomized a certain easy dressing in the 1950s, and became the core footwear of the preppy style, seen on women's feet as readily as on men's. Sebago, another major American footwear company, became Bass's main rival in the production of loafers.

Above and below: Tod's driving shoe – whether in classic leather or more colourful suede – is characterized by its distinctive rubber-studded sole, which has to be carefully set into the leather of the shoe by hand. **Opposite:** Michael Douglas, in about 1992, when he starred in Paul Verhoeven's *Basic Instinct*.

THE DRIVING SHOE

SHOES

With their supersoft construction they look more slipper than loafer, an impression that is only enhanced by the fact that they appear to be without a sole; this is replaced with serried ranks of 133 rubber nodules that curve distinctively up the heel and are coloured to match the leather. Certainly, the Tod's loafer – also known as the *gommino* (Italian for pebble) after its rubber studs – is some way from the penny loafer model popularized as part of America's 1950s Ivy League style.

It could not be anything other than Italian, both in style – somewhat louche, decadently casual in a *dolce vita* kind of way – and in sensibility; it was, after all, ostensibly designed as a shoe for driving, ideally something very fast and in a certain shade of red. Coincidentally, perhaps, Tod's founder, Diego Della Valle, has been a board member of both Ferrari and Maserati. And it was paparazzi shots of Gianni Agnelli, head of Fiat and an Italian style icon, wearing a pair of Tod's after he broke his leg skiing that sealed the style's success.

The *gommino* may have taken its inspiration from car shoes of the 1950s, but it has defined its category and spawned countless imitations. It also put an old family business on the map. Filippo, Diego's grandfather, was a leatherworker and shoemaker in the north Italian region of Le Marche, famous for its artisanal leather goods. Della Valle's father, Darino, expanded the business to produce high-end shoes for United States department stores, sold under their names. Della Valle joined it in 1975 after dropping out of law school in New York.

He concluded that the family business could be more successful if it made shoes under its own brand. The problem was how to stand out against the myriad other luxury Italian shoemakers. A signature style was required – one that might work for the more casual dressing that was then a distinctively American style but was slowly becoming a global one; a style that worked with a suit while simultaneously undercutting its propriety.

Della Valle found what he wanted four years later, in 1979, in the shape of an old driving shoe–loafer hybrid, a look that appealed to his interest in Ivy League style (in 1998 he bought John F. Kennedy's boat, *Marlin*, at auction). The brand name, originally J.P. Tod, was lifted from a Boston telephone directory and was chosen because it was easy to pronounce in any language and suggested an old family firm; when J.P. was dropped from the name the company received enquiries into the death of its patriarch. To drive home the American flavour of the Italian product, images of Cary Grant, Audrey Hepburn and Della Valle's own style hero, Steve McQueen, were used in advertising.

For the shoe itself, Della Valle simply added studs to the hybrid style and made it in the best leathers, most notably Vacchetta, a tan calfskin that is something of a signature. The pattern of holes in the leather sole, through which the studs protrude from a rubber panel, is cut by hand. The sole is sewn to the upper and the soft construction is then hand-moulded over a last and the stitched seams are hammered down – just a few of the 100 or so steps in the production process. It is a lot of work for an unostentatious product. But that, in part, is what has ensured its popularity.

THE BROGUE

SHOES

Punching holes through the toecaps of a pair of shoes to allow the insides to better dry out after they have been soaked (or so that feet can cool on a hot day) may be a blunt solution to a problem, but it gave rise to one of the most distinctive, and highly decorative, shoes in the male wardrobe: the brogue. The characteristic pits and serrated or 'gimped' edging are added to what is essentially a simple, closed-lacing Oxford or an open-lacing Derby style (also known as Bluchers, after Gebhard Leberecht von Blücher, the late-eighteenth century Prussian field marshal who popularized the shoe by ordering it for his troops). But, like many menswear classics, the brogue has its origins in utility.

It was Irish and Scottish agricultural workers, farming bogs and marshland, who in the sixteenth century first took an awl to their somewhat makeshift, heel-less shoes – *brogue* or *brog* means shoe in Gaelic – and created decorative patterns that were typical of the more flamboyant men's dress of the Elizabethan Age. Even as the style became more recognizably like the brogue of today, tackling the elements remained a key issue; the early shoes were made of leather shavings glued together, and were typically rubbed with candle wax to make them more water-repellent.

After some three centuries the decoration of the shoes remained, but their function was lost and the modern notion of brogues had been established. Even so, their country roots remained and the sturdy style was worn by gamekeepers until the turn of the twentieth century, when it was adopted by gentlemen – and then only for wear in the country, typically for sports. It was this association with the outdoors that led to a studded version of the brogue being taken up as a golf shoe, when Edward, Prince of Wales, broke yet another of the rules of dress etiquette (in this case that gentlemen wore only plain shoes) that so dominated society until the mid-twentieth century. The prince's influence during the 1920s in particular meant his radical views on fashion were adopted as the mainstream across Europe.

Opposite: The elegant dress to which the brogue lends itself is a long way from the Irish and Scottish bogs in which this style of shoe finds its origins.

Below and opposite: The classic English benchmade shoe – which the brogue has come to epitomize – is the product of some 200 separate operations; punching and placing its decorative holes involves even more. Factories such as this one, in Northamptonshire, England – the benchmade shoe's spiritual home – have been producing brogues since the mid-nineteenth century.

However, the brogue soon escaped its sporty connotations. It became fashionable in East European high society, thanks to handmade shoes from Budapest – and was also known as the Budapester. Arguably, it was the Prince of Wales, again, who first wore brogues on social occasions; he introduced the half-brogue (with a decorated toecap rather than the more expansive wingtip of a full brogue) and helped the style to move from country to city life.

The first black brogues were also seen at this time; until then tradition had dictated that they should be brown, in keeping with their country environment. This was only the first derivation for the brogue. With the wingtip separating a shoe's upper into delineated sections, two-tone (aka spectator or co-respondent) shoes followed, and helped to define the look of the Jazz Age, as well as the much-imitated dress sense of dancers Fred Astaire and Gene Kelly.

Brogues came to defy their humble origins, and by the 1940s were considered one of the more upmarket, dressier variants of men's shoes, made by companies such as Florsheim, established in Chicago in 1892, which built its reputation on the elegant wingtips with which its name would become synonymous. Small wonder that when Jack Nicolson's private detective J.J. Gittes is nearly drowned in a reservoir in *Chinatown* (1974), his chief concern is the loss of one of his shoes. 'Son of a bitch,' he says. 'That was a goddamn Florsheim shoe.'

THE DECK SHOE

SHOES

When deck shoes appeared on the cover of Lisa Birnbach's tongue-in-cheek *The Official Preppy Handbook* in 1980, it cemented their place in the upper-crust WASP wardrobe as the dressier alternative to sneakers – suggestive as they were of owning a yacht to wear them on. How fitting, then, that the readiness with which this shoe was taken up for its comfort and connotations – with countless versions on the market, of which some, such as Sebago, were more authentic than others – belied its debt to a prince. Of a kind.

The shoe's origins go back to the early 1930s when Paul Sperry, a one-time employee of Abercrombie & Fitch, learnt just how slippery the newly painted decks of a yacht can be. He had bought a rough-and-ready schooner and, after sprucing it up, set sail. But as soon as the decks became wet they were akin to an ice rink, and his sneakers offered little grip. So Sperry had an idea. Not to improve what he was wearing on his feet, but to improve the decks by repainting them with a layer of emery dust. This worked, at least in terms of providing grip. 'But if any part of the human anatomy came into touch with them, it was like giving yourself a rub down with sandpaper,' he explained.

He turned his attention to footwear. He rejected the espadrille-type shoes made by an English yachting company; they gave great traction when decks were wet but, ironically, their rope soles were slippery on dry surfaces. Instead, he conducted hundreds of experiments with rubber-soled shoes, none of which added up to much – until he noticed that his cocker spaniel, Prince, was able to handle slippery surfaces, and realized that what gave the dog's paws their grip was the tiny, multidirectional cracks that ran all over their pads. He took a more geometric but similar herringbone pattern and cut it into a rubber sole that he ran over his test bed – a sheet of polished metal.

The problem of slipping appeared to be resolved. An on-board trial of a prototype pair of shoes, worn by a young member of the schooner's crew, proved that the soles worked. Deck shoes had been invented. Sperry patented what he called the Razor-Siping design, and tried to sell the concept. He approached the United States Rubber Company, who decided the complex sole would price the shoes out of the market. Converse, however, was not so blinkered. From 1935 it made blank soles and shipped them to Sperry. He cut them and Converse finished the shoes.

Then marketing took over: Sperry's friend Donald White, an advertising man who worked for McGraw-Hill, came up with the name Sperry Top-Sider and persuaded him to sell the shoes (price $4.50) by mail order – a highly innovative sales medium at the time. Sperry sent handwritten letters to the 100 members of the prestigious Cruising Club of America. All of them wrote back. Word spread. One Mr Vanderbilt put in an order for the crew of his yacht, and Sperry struggled to meet orders for the shoes – even more so when in 1939, two years before the United States entered the Second World War, he won the contract to supply shoes to the US Navy. It stayed that way until he sold his interest in the business – to the United States Rubber Company.

But the story is not so easily resolved. Despite creating an icon, Sperry also sparked a debate that rages on. As the cover of *The Official Preppy Handbook* noted, Top-Siders are a 'crucial element' in preppy style. But they also pose what Birnbach called 'the sock controversy'. To wear, or not to wear – the argument has yet to be won.

Below: Examining a dog's paws gave Paul Sperry the idea for a new kind of grip for shoes to be worn on deck.

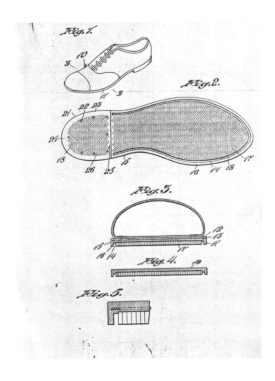

Above and right: The patent drawings for Sperry's design and an early prototype that he carved by hand.

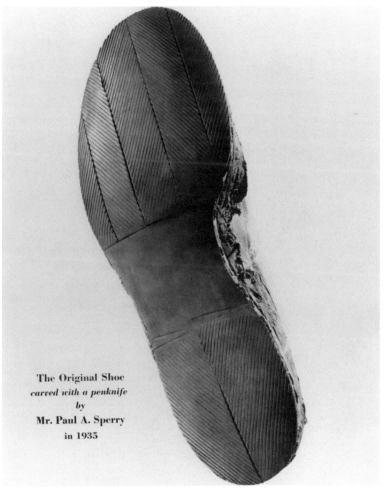

The Original Shoe
carved with a penknife
by
Mr. Paul A. Sperry
in 1935

4.
UNDERWEAR

Y-FRONTS / THE T-SHIRT /
BOXER SHORTS

Y-FRONTS

UNDERWEAR

Opposite: Mike Tyson with his pet tiger, one of six he owned. Below: Modelling underwear was once so risqué that the models wore black masks to hide their identities. Bottom: As late as 1938, Cooper's Underwear Company (Jockey's predecessor) had to devise ways of promoting Y-fronts without showing them too explicitly; in one example it staged a wedding in which the bride and groom, both wearing Jockeys, were covered – ineffectively – with sheets of cellophane.

The first commercial for Jockey Y-fronts aired on America's *The Tonight Show* in 1958, a time when chat-show hosts were expected to present promotional slots in person and live. The honour fell to Jack Paar, who fell into fits of laughter as he held up the underwear and read his script from the boards. The client was not pleased. But the planned 30-second commercial lasted two minutes while Paar recovered himself and started again, and the next day there was a run on Jockey briefs across the United States.

Compared to the simplicity of boxer shorts there is something comical about Y-fronts. And this is despite their obvious functional advantages: a snug fit and support. The name Jockey suggested sleek lines and the top-drawer image of equestrianism – and was also a way of hinting at 'jock strap' (the sports device and then the only way for men to find support) without using what was then deemed an offensive term.

It was in 1934 that Arthur Kneibler, an executive of Cooper's Underwear Company (Jockey's predecessor), received a postcard from the French Riviera depicting a man wearing a bikini-style swimsuit. This gave him an idea: to replace loose-fit boxers with a daringly skimpy brief that, as promotional material coyly had it, offered 'comfortable and masculine support'.

During the year it took to get the new design to market, the prototype was refined in consultation with a medical specialist in urinary tracts and underwent considerable testing. On 19 January 1935 the first briefs were unveiled in Chicago's Marshall Field & Co. department store. All 600 sold out in three hours. The following week 12,000 were bought and Jockey had to hire an aircraft, wittily dubbed the 'Masculiner', to speed up national distribution.

At the end of 1935 Jockey introduced an evolution of the brief: the fly opening. This comprised two overlapping flaps, the seams of which created a Y-shape, and not only allowed 'improved masculine access' – a delicate point to get across at the time – but was also a clever piece of engineering. In Jockey's original briefs, seams that ran up the front of each leg provided the main support. The Y-front, which originally sold for 50 cents, shifted the direction of the truss work and redistributed weight, as one sales bulletin of the time had it, to 'the upright portion of the letter which is attached to the elastic belt of the garment'. In short, the wearer could position the waistband where it was most comfortable and gave the desired level of support. This also allowed Jockey to develop versions of the Y-front with, for example, legs. In 1959 the company launched the first low-rise bikini underwear for men, made of 100 per cent stretch nylon – one of the new synthetic wonder fabrics of the decade

The Y-front's history can be traced to another part of the anatomy: the feet. Samuel T. Cooper was on holiday in Minnesota in 1876 when he met lumberjacks suffering from foot sores, largely due to ill-fitting and poor quality socks. Unable to convince sock manufacturers to improve their product, he launched his own company. At the turn of the twentieth century Cooper's branched out into underwear with its White Cat brand, which was as pioneering as Jockey would be later. In 1909, at a time when men wore 'drop seat' all-in-one union suits, with an inconvenient and uncomfortable panel at the rear, one of its designers, Horace Greely Johnson, was responsible for a style with an overlapping diagonal opening at the front – not dissimilar to that used in the Y-front. The Kenosha Klosed Krotch became the international template for men's underwear, much as the Jockey styles were a generation later.

THE T-SHIRT

UNDERWEAR

The T-shirt may not be the oldest garment in the male wardrobe, but arguably it can lay claim to being the simplest. It is also one of the most potent – a blank canvas for branding, art and political comment. But long before graphic designer Milton Glaser created the 'I ♥ NY' graphic, before Alberto Korda's photograph of Che Guevara graced a million chests, the T-shirt was a humble, and hidden, piece of underwear.

Male underwear was traditionally a union suit, an all-in-one undergarment that combined body, long sleeves and ankle-length leggings. It was the end of the nineteenth century before two-piece underwear – a long-sleeved shirt and long johns, often buttoned together – came into vogue. Keeping the entire body warm was deemed essential for warding off cold-related illnesses, which is why undergarments were made of wool and men rarely dispensed with their jacket or waistcoat even indoors.

The T-shirt had its origins in military requirements. In about 1913 amendments to the uniforms of both the Royal Navy and the United States Navy meant British servicemen wore a vest-type undergarment and American seamen a cropped-sleeve undershirt – an evolution of the square-necked, shoulder-buttoning shirt worn since the 1880s. The changes were ostensibly made to leave men's arms free when they performed deck chores or manned armaments. White (still the T-shirt's most popular colour) was chosen for several reasons: it married well with the colours of navy uniforms, it was cheap to manufacture as it required no dyeing, and since it revealed dirt it helped to instil self-discipline and maintain hygiene. The problem was that the British garment offered little protection and the American one was made of wool flannelette and took a long time to dry.

Two companies in particular led the development of the T-shirt as it is now recognized. Before the First World War a United Kingdom manufacturer, Thomas A. Hill and Co. – established in the late nineteenth century and later known as Sunspel – had exported long-sleeved but lightweight cotton underwear to tropical climates, notably to Britain's colonies in the Far East. Meanwhile, an

Opposite: Paul Newman as 'Fast' Eddie Felson in *The Hustler* (1961). **Below:** Sailors playing cards below decks on a US Navy vessel during the Second World War; the plain white T-shirt was part of their standard uniform, but was not issued to US Army personnel until after the war.

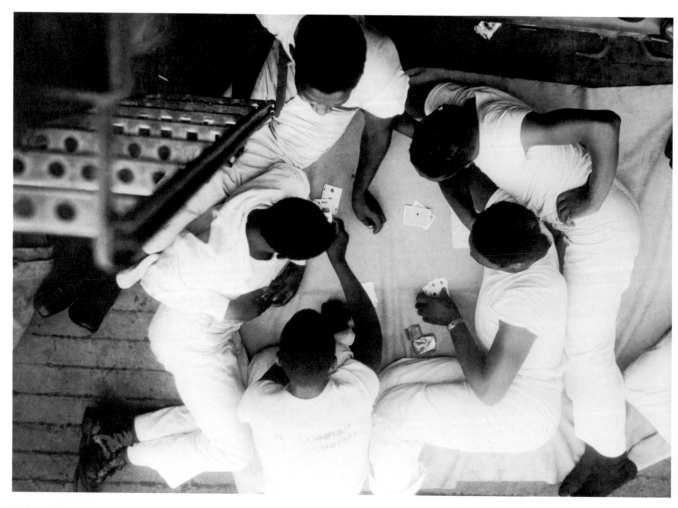

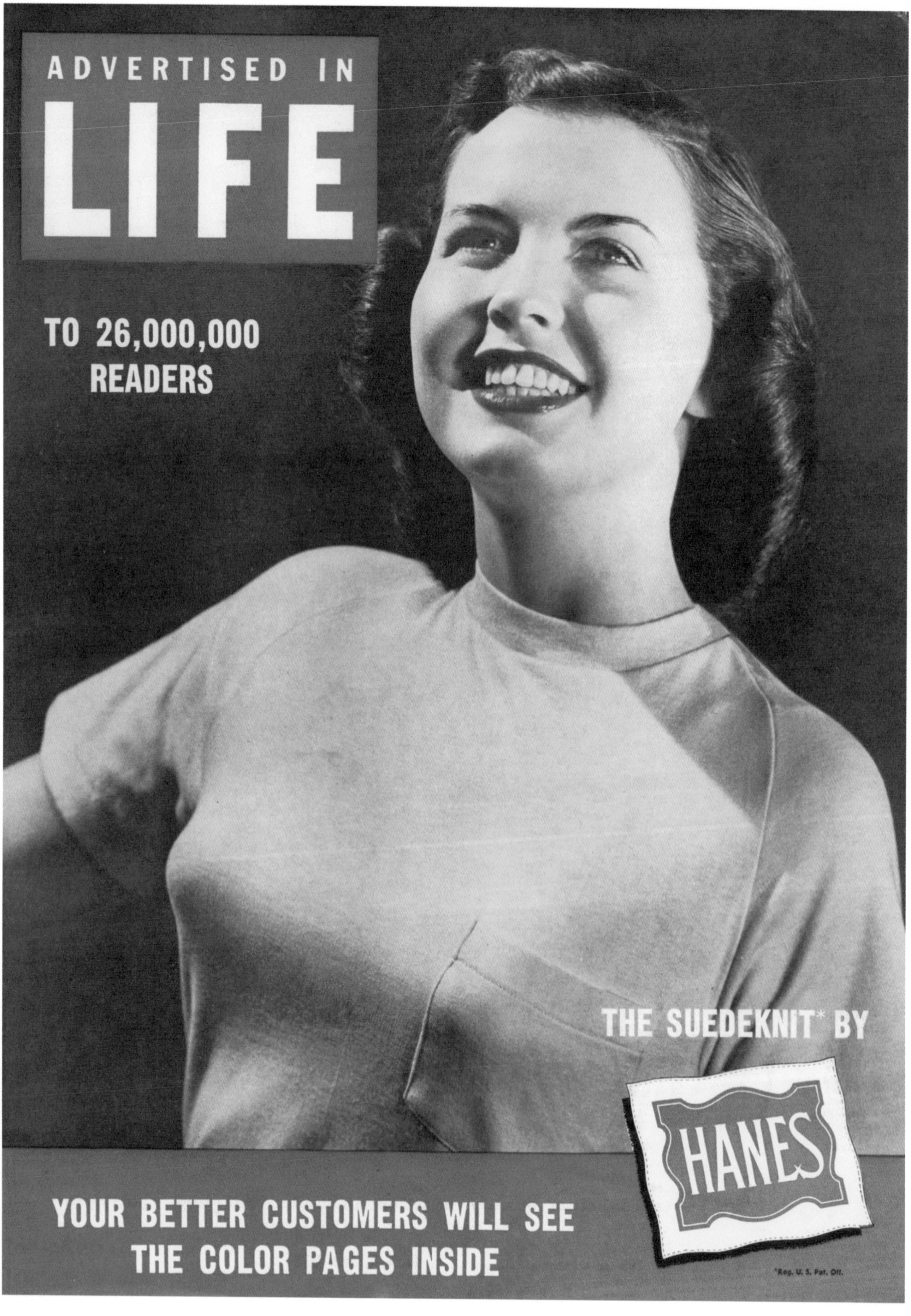

ADVERTISED IN
LIFE

TO 26,000,000
READERS

THE SUEDEKNIT* BY

HANES

YOUR BETTER CUSTOMERS WILL SEE
THE COLOR PAGES INSIDE

*Reg. U. S. Pat. Off.

American fabric merchant, Jacob Goldfarb, was selling, under the Fruit of the Loom brand, an evolution of a T-shirt-type garment he had been making since 1910. When British and American soldiers met in the trenches the idea of combining a cotton fabric with short sleeves was born. The other major T-shirt manufacturer, Hanes, creator of the Beefy T, entered the market in about 1930. It was the first company to produce T-shirts for promotional purposes – specifically, for the release of *The Wizard of Oz* in 1939.

The popularity of the simple T-shirt grew in the run-up to the United States' entry into the Second World War: a Sears, Roebuck and Co. advertisement proclaimed, 'You needn't be in the army to have your own personal t-shirt', suggesting the item was fast becoming indicative of a certain heroism or machismo. Nevertheless, wearing an uncovered T-shirt did not become socially acceptable until after the war, when public resistance had been worn down by images of soldiers at work and unconcerned with propriety. In July 1942, six months after the bombing of Pearl Harbor, the cover of *Life* magazine featured a trainee at the Air Corps Gunnery School wearing a T-shirt, with the institution's name emblazoned across its front. The white T-shirt became an official part of the US Army duty uniform only after the war, and was later dyed khaki to make it less obvious to enemy fire.

By the mid-1950s the T-shirt had become the symbol of the new teenager and of rock 'n' roll rebellion. It was sported sweat-soaked and sexually magnetic by Marlon Brando in *A Streetcar Named Desire* (1951) and under tough-guy leather in *The Wild One* (1953); and as the cool uniform of James Dean and jazz trumpeter Chet Baker.

Opposite: The Suedeknit T-shirt became one of Hanes' best-selling styles after the Second World War. Indeed, it rapidly became an everyman and everywoman product. 'On their precious vacation dates, Dad and Mom will really relax – in Hanes Suedeknit Sports Shirts,' ran another advertisement in 1948. 'So comfortable – yet you look and feel "well dressed" for any resort occasion.' **Right:** Other advertisements treated the T-shirt as an ideal undergarment.

BOXER SHORTS

UNDERWEAR

Few sartorial rivalries are as distinct as that between boxer shorts – the male wardrobe's most classic undergarment – and Y-front briefs. The battle has even resulted in scientifically unproven claims that 'masculine support', as Jockey, creator of the Y-front, once put it, was essential to a healthy sperm count, while the opposition had it that boxer shorts' better regulation of the temperature around the genitals had an equally beneficial effect.

Nor has the stand-off been without its ironies. Tastes may change – the preference for Y-fronts during the 1970s suffered an abrupt about-turn in 1984, thanks to Levi's model Nick Kamen being seen in pristine white boxers for one of its 501 jeans cinema campaigns. But surveys have repeatedly found that, at the turn of the twenty-first century at least, something like two men out of three prefer briefs to boxers – the female preference is the inverse.

Woven cotton, knitted or broadcloth boxer shorts were first popular some time after 1926 when Jacob Golomb founded Union Underwear and later the sports brand Everlast. He provided boxers (of the fighting kind) with new, lighter, more comfortable elastic-waisted shorts to replace the leather-belted versions that had been worn until then. By the 1930s the rising demand for comfort saw a fashion craze for versions of the boxers' shorts that could be worn as underwear. Golomb manufactured them under licence with Fruit of the Loom, which dates to 1871 and is one of America's oldest brands.

As well as providing relief from the heavy, mostly wool underwear that preceded them, boxer shorts also introduced sartorial interest through the variety of patterned or shirting fabrics that were used to make them. Some, such as the 'atomic' prints of the 1950s and the novelty shorts of the late 1980s, were barometers of their times; others, like the brightly coloured silk boxers popular in the United States during the early 1930s, were said to provide men with an escape from the woes of the Great Depression; there was some colour under their otherwise dour exteriors.

Opposite: Often cited as the greatest boxer of all time, and welterweight champion from 1946 to 1950, Sugar Ray Robinson – with Omaha boxer Vince Foster – wearing the original Everlast boxer shorts. **Below right:** A 1960s novelty print pair of boxer shorts from Fruit of the Loom.

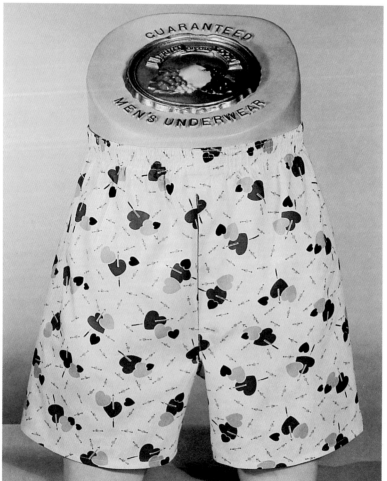

Early boxer shorts were effectively truncated and looser versions of long johns, named after John L. Sullivan, the American boxer popular during the 1880s. More sophisticated models had the added benefit of what was known as a balloon seat – a panel of extra fabric in the rear of the shorts that allowed movement without the boxers pulling against the body. Long johns remained commonplace in the United States until the 1930s, and in the United Kingdom until 1947 when John Hill of the British brand Sunspel introduced boxer shorts after a visit to America. Their rapid popularity might be attributed to the GIs who were stationed in Britain (and other countries) during the Second World War: boxer shorts had been standard issue.

During the war, while boxers with elasticated waists and metal snap closures had long been on the market, an old-style tie-side version – the tapes on each hip could be tightened and knotted – with button fastenings was reintroduced to spare rubber and metal for the war effort. This was just one of many devices that ensured a comfortable fit; others included the elastic-free French Back, which featured a series of buttons with a tab that could be tightened. Styles were also devised to protect the wearer's modesty, notably the uppermost layer of the fly was cut at a diagonal to the waistband. But men have always been too conscious of the need for easy access for the fly opening itself to be a new idea. It dates back to the Renaissance, when a button or tie-closing opening was cut into *braies* – calf-length underwear worn by men since the thirteenth century.

Opposite: Nick Kamen disrobes in 1984's Levi's advertisement. **Below:** Boxer shorts gave men the opportunity to explore a variety of prints, colours and materials that remained less socially acceptable in outerwear.

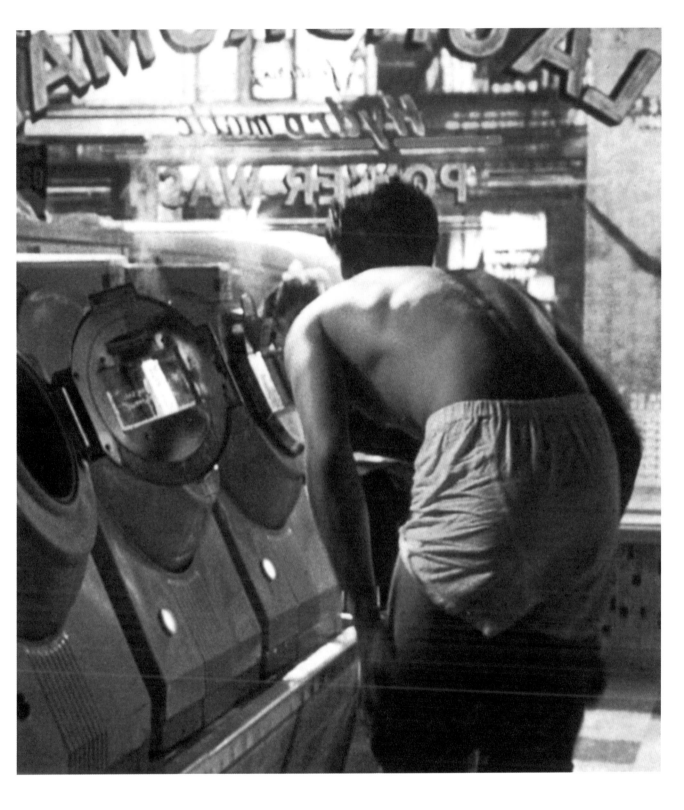

5.
TAILORING

THE BESPOKE SUIT / THE DINNER SUIT / THE SACK SUIT / THE BLAZER / THE READY-TO-WEAR SUIT / THE TWEED JACKET

THE BESPOKE SUIT

TAILORING

Perhaps no other garment typifies the apogee of men's style more than the bespoke suit – made by hand, and from scratch, for the individual; designed with a tailor's eye to hide the wearer's physical weaknesses and make the most of his attributes; magnifying masculinity; its sombre shades the epitome of formality. Unlike other icons of the male wardrobe, it did not originate with one company, nor was it designed to suit a particular need. The suit, as the heart of menswear, is a garment of evolution.

The English king Charles II took to wearing a long jacket, waistcoat and breeches – the basis of the modern suit – in the late seventeenth century, at a time when war with Holland had left the national coffers at rock bottom and a new frugality was in order. The garments were made from dark, matching fabrics and as a result Charles's courtiers were forced to stop wearing the rich materials and flamboyant finery that characterized the dress of any man with enough money to buy new clothing. This change was more radical than it may seem today: not only did the aristocracy define fashion but clothes were an expression of status and wealth. To dress darkly was to dress like the masses and was, arguably, the first step towards the democratization of the suit. A further step, by the eighteenth century, was to adapt clothing to make riding more comfortable by shortening the jacket, cutting it away from the front, making the whole ensemble closer fitting and tailoring it in warm wool; unbuttoning, and turning back, the top button prefigured jacket lapels.

The English gentleman-about-town George 'Beau' Brummell, and his fanatical attention to how his clothes fitted (more tightly than ever before), brought the suit even closer to the kind that is worn today. Such was Brummell's command over perceptions of correct dress in early nineteenth-century fashionable society – not to mention the influence he wielded, thanks to his on–off companionship with his 'fat friend' the Prince Regent, later George IV – that by 1824 Beethoven was bemoaning his lack of a black coat to wear for the première of his Ninth Symphony in Vienna. Brummell's influence during the

Opposite: Clark Gable poses for a publicity shot in the late 1930s; the jacket's peaked lapels and the high-waisted trousers are characteristic of the period. The court of Charles II introduced jackets for men that buttoned up right to left – this enabled a right-handed man to unfasten or fasten his jacket with his left hand while leaving his right hand free to draw his sword. Charles also introduced matching dark jackets and trousers. War with Holland had left the national coffers empty and a new era of frugality was required. Right: Catwalk moments for Savile Row tailor Hardy Amies.

nineteenth century's first two decades also saw suits that were 'bespoken' for an individual: they were made for him, in terms of both his form and his fancy. Influenced by country sports and the needs of military men, the suit as it is known today was effectively established by the twentieth century.

Although bespoke tailoring is not quintessentially British, and it probably originated in medieval France – 'tailor' is derived from *tailler* (to cut) – it was London's Savile Row area that came to be recognized as its spiritual home: the Japanese take their word for a suit, *sabburu*, from the street name. It was where the great and good had their suits made. The making of the first one was a rite of passage, with its dozen or more personal measurements, the discussion of cloth, cut and details, the making up of a pattern, and the several fittings required to perfect the final garment. Here the likes of Anderson & Sheppard, Gieves & Hawkes, Henry Poole and Huntsman & Sons are among the oldest and most esteemed names – with, latterly, more directional ones such as Tommy Nutter, Hardy Amies and Douglas Hayward.

Historically, the old guard have been the most protective of tradition. For instance, two developments in the 1930s – belted trousers and the trouser zip – were widely considered too radical. Traditionalists thought belts spoilt the manner in which trousers hang. And only Lord Louis Mountbatten favouring the zip saw the contraption reluctantly adopted.

The periods before and after the Second World War saw the first high-quality ready-to-wear suits available on a truly mass scale, with bespoke tailoring increasingly for the elite. By the turn of the twenty-first century, however, Savile Row had taken a more commercial, customer-friendly approach. Several new companies that were as au fait with marketing as they were with cutting and sewing opened shop and gave bespoke tailoring a new, more fashionable and accessible lease of life, especially in the face of the increased casualness of men's dress.

Opposite: Hardy Amies, the impeccably dressed Savile Row tailor and couturier to Elizabeth II. Tailoring first came to the Savile Row area in London thanks to Robert Baker, who set up the first tailoring business in the late sixteenth century in nearby Piccadilly – the name is itself derived from 'pickadil', a shirt collar of the Elizabethan era. **Below:** The tailors' art – the best cutting is as much about instinct as accuracy.

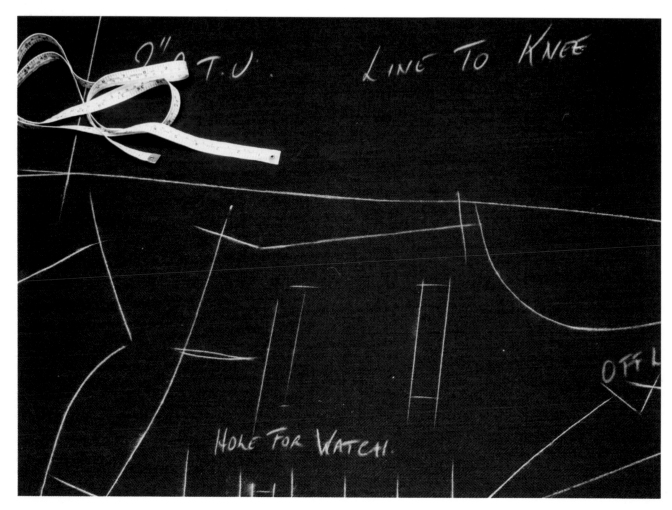

THE DINNER SUIT

TAILORING

The dinner suit is a curio in the male wardrobe: a specialist item, yet designed more for effect than function; expensive, yet rarely worn; supremely elegant and beloved by Lotharios and James Bond, yet giving little opportunity for self-expression. While it has evolved by small degrees since its arrival in the mid-nineteenth century, the dinner suit today is much as it was then: a fitted jacket with slit pockets, one-button fastening and – its most distinctive feature – a silk-, velvet- or grosgrain-covered shawl collar or, from the early twentieth century, a jacket with more military peak lapels; matching trousers; white wing-collared shirt; and neat bow tie.

It has been suggested that dressing for dinner came about because upper-class gentlemen whose clothes were grubby from activities on their estates needed to change. Influenced by menswear's love of black – from Beau Brummell's rejection of finery, through to Victorian practicality and Protestant restraint – dinner dress was originally an adaptation of military uniform, rendered in the colour of the night. The white shirt was starched and worn with a matching bow tie and a waistcoat, topped with a cutaway silk-lapelled jacket or tailcoat (as worn for riding) and trousers with a braided seam (as in uniforms of the day). Called 'full dress', the ensemble is worn today on especially formal occasions.

A shorter 'dinner jacket' infiltrated evening events, via the smoking jacket, and finally evolved into a new, more relaxed take on full dress. Queen Victoria's eldest son, the future Edward VII, adopted the look in 1860 and ensured its place in polite society. In 1886 the New York millionaire and coffee broker James Brown Potter, a guest of the prince, emulated him and introduced the style to the members of Tuxedo Park, a private country club for wealthy New Yorkers – from which the dinner suit (aka evening suit or 'black tie') takes its more informal name: the tuxedo.

While elitists prefer the term dinner jacket, tuxedo was commonly used in the United States. In Europe the jacket became known as the Monte Carlo – perhaps as a consequence of it being worn in Monaco's famed casinos – or,

Opposite: Fred Astaire may be the most famous wearer of top hat and tails, but Sean Connery as James Bond must be the most famous wearer of the classic dinner suit. Here he strikes the pose re-created in the poster for *From Russia With Love* (1963). **Below:** Bob Hope, on the right, in black tie. **Bottom:** Cary Grant, on the left, in white tie, alongside his wife, Virginia Cherrill, and Randolph Scott. **Right:** The dinner suit is arguably the most glamorous item in a man's wardrobe, an association from which advertisers have often tried to benefit.

especially in France, *le smoking*, reflecting the style's historical connection to the smoking jacket.

Whatever its name, by the 1920s the dinner suit had democratized eveningwear, inasmuch as tails were rarely worn and the style was suitable for most functions. Its adoption by Prince Edward, international trend-setter and future Duke of Windsor, more or less guaranteed its wide acceptance as the standard in dinner dress. The prince introduced twists of his own, most notably the use of midnight blue, rather than black, fabric, and a backless, white piqué waistcoat – a bib held together 'behind the scenes' by two straps.

Later changes to the standard style included the abandonment, in the 1930s, of the waistcoat (the cummerbund, although widely considered gimmicky, sometimes took its place); the adoption of the Marcella, a semi-stiff-fronted or pleat-fronted shirt (with a turn-down collar and cuffs in the waistcoat's piqué); and lighter fabrics. Variations such as double-breasted jackets, white jackets for warmer weather and colour co-ordinated accessories have been more fad than properly formal.

Attempts were later made to introduce an element of fashion and, perhaps, individualize the conformity of what was supra-fashion and adherence to dress etiquette. The 1950s and 1960s saw jackets in loud colours, patterns and textured fabrics – silk-faced lapels retained some formality – and experimentation with ties such as the continental crossover, a silk strip that overlapped where the knot had been and was held together with a button. 1970s fashions included dramatic, Edwardian flourishes and cuts, even Nehru jackets. Small wing collars and red accessories appeared in the 1990s, and the 2000s was the era of notch lapels and the so-called 'creative black tie'. However, the style established by the 1930s continues to define the classic and, one might say, the most legitimate 'black tie'.

Below: A Huntsman dinner suit with both a double-breasted jacket and a shawl collar – one of the many combinations with which dinner dress has experimented. **Opposite:** The peak-lapelled dinner suit of the 1930s and 1940s was arguably the best of all variations.

THE SACK SUIT

TAILORING

The turn of the twentieth century saw a radical new development in menswear. Until then, most gentlemen's clothing was custom-made or custom-ordered; the idea that someone could walk into a store with a wallet and walk out with clothing was a bold departure from the norm. Brooks Brothers has attributed much of its early success to its then innovative emphasis on ready-made clothing – it sourced its own fabrics and operated its own workshops.

Manufacturing ready-made garments meant that the company became the designer, with decisions about dress and style made for the customer rather than by him, and was consequently a definer of style and shaper of society. Perhaps the most profound example of this was the impact on tailoring. Until 1900 men generally had their suits – stiff, hard-wearing and precision-fitting – made for them. But in this year Brooks Brothers introduced its Number One 'sack suit'. Its rather unflattering name was at least accurate: Brooks brought the baggy clothing that had been worn by the average man for some decades to tailoring. The suit had a softer construction, a 'natural', padding-free shoulder, a comfortable, four-button jacket (a three-button was launched in 1918) with a centre vent and a buttonhole in the left lapel, and straight, loose trousers.

It was, in a way, the first case of deconstruction. More casual, comfortable clothing was a fashion choice rather than indicating that someone was indifferent to what they wore. The suit was widely imitated and set the basic style for American menswear, and business dress in particular, for at least the next five decades; the protagonist of *The Man in the Grey Flannel Suit* (1956), in which Gregory Peck's character epitomizes the anonymity of office life and corporate America, wore a style that is a clear descendant of the sack suit. So, too, is the characteristic Italian fashion suiting of the late 1970s and early 1980s when Giorgio Armani was said to be (re-)releasing men from the strictures of traditional tailoring. Pedestrian as the sack suit style may look today, when it was introduced it extended boundaries, less as a disposable fashion – something to which Brooks Brothers was opposed – and more as a progressive, functional way of dressing.

When Brooks moved away from the Number One sack suit cut it did so largely out of desperation. During the Great Depression, in a bid to increase sales, it had displayed the suit, complete with price tag, in its store windows as a totem of what later would be called its brand identity; what was then regarded as aggressive marketing scandalized the company's regulars, and the suits were soon removed. Later in the 1930s, in another bid to encourage customers to buy, Brooks introduced the Number Two suit, with a nipped-in waist and broad, padded shoulders. One writer of the time called it 'a ghastly concession to hard times'. Tellingly, when trade picked up, the company quickly modified the style along Number One lines.

As *The New Yorker* put it in 1938, the sack suit is 'the real trademark of Brooks Brothers. Brought up-to-date every year or so, it nevertheless essentially hasn't changed in half a century. The coat has been copied time and time again by other tailors, but the true Brooks fanatic insists upon the natural shoulders, the distinctive roll of the lapels, the straight lines, the general uncompromising sloppiness of the general article.' And the reference to sloppiness was a compliment. The sack suit, as the article went on, 'remains a whole philosophy of dress'.

Opposite: Gregory Peck is measured up in 1956's *The Man in the Grey Flannel Suit*. **Below:** The style of Brooks Brothers' sack suit was a radical departure from the traditional tailoring of the time, indicative of a company that knew even men's suiting had to keep evolving. 'If we were thoroughly conservative, we'd be dead,' a Brooks Brothers executive said in the 1950s.

THE BLAZER

TAILORING

The blazer has long seemed most at home with the old school tie and a certain hauteur. The kind of semiformal tailoring worn on yachts or at polo matches, it is the jacket of respectability donned by David Niven in *Death on the Nile* (1978) or the cinematic James Bond in *The Man with the Golden Gun* (1974), rather than that of practical, shabby seafaring as worn by Humphrey Bogart in *Key Largo* (1948).

While the blazer is typically teamed with chinos and loafers for casual smartness, it finds its origins in the disciplined environment of the Royal Navy. Before the introduction of blue and white dress regulations for all servicemen, it was not unknown for captains to decide on the look of their crews' uniforms. During the mid-nineteenth century this loose arrangement allowed Captain Wilmott of HMS *Harlequin* to pay for his men to wear harlequin outfits and the captain of HMS *Vernon* to order his to wear red serge frocks; when stock ran out only the port watch dressed in red and the starboard wore navy. So in 1837, when the captain of HMS *Blazer* heard that the new queen, Victoria, would inspect his ship, he smartened up his crew by making them wear blue-and-white striped seamen's sweaters and navy-blue jackets in a short, black-buttoned, double-breasted reefer style – 'reefing' the sails reduces the area of sail exposed to the wind.

That is one story, and the double-breasted, side-vented, navy-blue blazer certainly became part of the nautical fashion inspired by Britain's nineteenth-century naval power and empire-building. There is a clear lineage to HMS *Blazer*'s jackets: the reefer evolved to become a longer style with six gold buttons, worn as part of an officer's dress uniform. So-called monkey jackets, with eight buttons, worn on active duty are similar, and army regiments adopted the style (often in shades of green) for unofficial wear at civilian events. Another story is that the style originated with the jackets worn by members of the Lady Margaret Boat Club of St John's College, Cambridge – they were an eye-watering red, suggesting their wearers were on fire, and so were called 'blazers'.

The style became known as a boating jacket and, in turn, as one for sports, mainly tennis and cricket, at a time when players' uniforms were less specialized than they are today and more hidebound by sartorial rules. In this context, blazers were as bold as team strips in order to differentiate teammate from opposition: although the traditional double-breasted blazer in block navy is now the standard, on earlier, single-breasted versions bold stripes or distinctive contrast piping for lapels and cuffs were common in the United Kingdom.

This style became part of the British public school uniforms of the Edwardian era, complete with badge or crest on the breast pocket and a matching peaked cap or boater. 'The striped flannel jackets, under the familiar name "blazer", brilliant in colouring, created for the river and the cricket field, are worn on nearly all occasions now by girls and boys,' a commentator in the *Lady's World* journal noted in 1887. Blazers were often awarded as a mark of sporting or academic excellence, or membership of an august institution of higher learning. Perhaps this association with certain elites is why they were appropriated by the mods of the 1960s: members of The Who, The Kinks, The Yardbirds and The Animals, among other key groups of the era, often dressed more as though they were about to attend Henley Regatta than trash the stage.

Left: George V in full naval uniform, the blazer's fitted form and polished buttons providing a swagger that the uniforms of other services lacked. This is surely the heart of its appeal when it is worn in civilian life, something the Roger Moore-era James Bond movies reflected.

Bracken Twist worsted, made to measure £32.

Town suit or country suit—
it depends which shirt you're wearing.

Just think how useful a suit from the Burton Town and Country range would be to you.

Swop your shirt for a sweater, or a different type of shirt, and you're dressed for a different way of life.

Take the one shown here. It's a fine Bracken Twist worsted in a glen check.

You can wear it to the office without looking as if you've just come off the farm. Wear it in a country pub, and you could be taken for one of the better-dressed rural types.

You get Burton Town and Country suits made to measure or ready to wear. Either way, it's like getting two suits for the price of one. Prices start at £16.

And with a couple in your wardrobe, you're ready for anything—anywhere.

Burton
Colourful things are going on.

26

Above: An advertisement for Burton's Town and Country range from the early 1970s, when the idea of dressing differently for urban and rural settings was still prevalent.

THE READY-TO-WEAR SUIT

TAILORING

'To his tailor no man is a hero,' read a newspaper advertisement of the early 1950s, complete with an illustration of a man in a neat two-button, single-breasted, three-piece suit. 'Overall statistics from the records of Montague Burton Ltd, the world's largest tailoring organisation, produce this picture of The Average Man. His height is 5ft 9in and he has a slight tendency towards rounded shoulders. He boasts a 38-inch chest measurement and a 35-inch waist. His arms are 32 inches long and his legs are 30 and three-quarter inches (inside measurement)...'.

Montague Burton's company, later known simply as Burton's and still going strong, was among the first to offer the average man the kind of tailoring that had previously been available only to the wealthy. If bespoke tailors cut for the singular man and charged accordingly, Burton made suits that hid most sins and cost considerably less. In effect, he helped to democratize the suit and pave the way for today's ready-to-wear versions.

This had been his mission when in 1903, aged 18 and with £100 borrowed from a relative, he opened the Cross-Tailoring Company in Chesterfield in England, with the promise that men could replace their cotton or moleskin working clothes or hand-me-downs with a made-to-measure suit offered at an accessible price and in a new style that was equally at home in town or country, for factory or office work.

He fufilled his promise not least by adopting what were radically humanistic employment policies: fair wages, workers' rights and progressive working conditions, including Europe's first air-conditioned factory and largest canteen. He also divided tailoring labour so that a customer could have a suit made from scratch and delivered in 24 hours, and instituted vertical integration. Then a revolutionary idea, this meant controlling the production process from weaving through to manufacture and sales, and eliminated profits that would otherwise be made by intermediary companies.

Below: Pages from Burton's catalogues of the 1940s and 1950s display the broad spread of styles that was possible even with early mass-manufactured tailoring – what the pioneering Burton called 'multiple tailoring'. He was opposed to what he referred to as 'style monotony – where would the automobile industry and drapery business be if the 1920s models were still in vogue? Modern tailoring methods [mean] men are able to afford a greater change and variety of attire, which tends to develop a race of well-dressed men. And the immaculate citizen is an asset to his community.'

D.B. Suit style expressing flawlessly one of the best ideas and designs in dress for men. Elegant and beautifully fashioned. Delights and satisfies. Tailored to your own measurements from a superb range of new "Oceanic" Weaves . . . . (see the companion page)

5 GUINEA VALUE
D.B. SUIT
TO-MEASURE FOR 55/-

Such dignity for City wear, such grace . . . the last word in correct appearance . . . cut in black worsted of plain or fancy weave, with worsted trousers of striped pattern. A triumph in Tasteful Tailoring, correct in every detail.

No business man can secure a better bargain

5 GUINEA VALUE
SUIT - TO-MEASURE
BLACK JACKET AND VEST
WITH STRIPED TROUSERS
for 55/-

During the First World War some 25 per cent of British soldiers wore uniforms made by Burton's company. This gave it the financial footing to expand massively, so that by 1928 it was operating some 400 shops, factories and mills across the United Kingdom and served the entire British Empire. In his book *Ideals in Industry*, published in 1925, Burton opined that the war, along with a general societal overhaul, had been the making of the modern suit: regional and professionally distinct styles of dress 'underwent a swift and radical change'.

In time, Burton suits became part of the social fabric of Britishness, not least because they were long-lasting; each cloth and style underwent rigorous tests, including rubbing, simulated downpours, exposure to sunlight, and soaking the sleeve linings in a solution that was described in *Ideals in Industry* as being 'equivalent to that of the perspiration produced by an average man after standing continuously in a hot atmosphere for 145 minutes'.

When the Second World War ended Burton supplied all servicemen with clothes, including a three-piece suit, for their return to civilian life. This demob (from demobilization) suit was nicknamed 'the full Monty' – what would become slang for 'the whole thing' or 'everything that is wanted or needed'. By 1950 one in five men in the United Kingdom wore a Burton suit every day, and in 1966 the company provided England's World Cup football champions with their suits. By then, thanks to Burton's pioneering, ready-to-wear tailoring was a widespread reality.

Opposite and below: More pages from Burton's early catalogues. The company aimed to offer what Burton suggested was 'a five guinea suit for 55 shillings'. This was made possible by complete control of the production process. As the company proclaimed, 'several intermediary profits are eliminated, and these profits, with all the economies and benefits made possible by the Largest Tailoring Organisation in the World, are passed on to you'. 'One of the miracles in my lifetime is wrought by Montague Burton,' as the writer of the spring 1939 *Tailoring of Taste* brochure had it. 'Every man can now enjoy the satisfaction of being well-dressed because of what that great firm has done.'

For holiday resorts, for the beach and promenade, for business wear in the summer months, there's no suit cooler to wear, cooler to look at, so comfortably graceful, as this well-tailored Montague Burton Flannel. Fashioned to retain its shape in the hottest suns. Double-breasted style from specially selected all-wool Flannel in the latest shades of Grey, and stripes

Leisure, those idle care-free re-creating moments, has brought the Lounge Sports Jacket and Flannel Trousers into great popularity
Colourful and yet restful are these jackets, for lounge and sports, tailored in cheerful plaid and checkered weaves of the kind which men like and enjoy as they enjoy a favourite pipe or book. Stylishly tailored . . . single or double breasted . . . free swing and shirred backs, half-belt . . . in fancy check patterns. Ideal ensemble worn with "University" flannel trousers, in latest shades, fitted with extension waistband, adjustable side straps, semi-cross pockets, finished with pleated waist
Complete outfit for 40/- . . . is there any value to compare with it? It's the gold standard in men's tailoring

4 GUINEA VALUE
D.B. FLANNEL SUIT
TO MEASURE FOR 45/-

2 GUINEA VALUE
LOUNGE SPORTS JACKET
ready to-wear for 25/-

1 GUINEA VALUE
WORSTED FLANNEL TROUSERS
ready to-wear for 15/-

Page 8

Page 17

"Laird" Scotch Tweed Plus-Four Suit possesses a rugged strength in wear and a proved loyalty in service like a trusted friend faithful in all weathers. If you are hard on your clothes, here's your choice . . And you'll wonder that so much beauty of pattern, so much delicacy of style can be combined with rigour of service. As smart as it is sturdy, as delightful as it is durable . . . as popular as its price

5 GUINEA VALUE
PLUS FOUR SUIT
TO MEASURE FOR 55/-

Page 18

THE TWEED JACKET

TAILORING

The single-breasted two-button tweed jacket is a quintessentially British garment – and a contradictory one. Rough to the touch, it is tailored yet often sloppy. It suggests the upper-class country-house set but was adopted by 1950s radicals; it is smart enough to go almost anywhere, yet is sturdy enough to be worn around mud and muck. The tweed jacket is Prince Charles carrying a shotgun – and Woody Allen wearing battered cords.

Tweed itself is the story behind the jacket. It was first made in Scotland, and is the generic name for a flecked woollen fabric that was carded and spun by hand, woven, and then stretched and dried before being cut and sewn. Thornproof and naturally water repellent, its thickest versions can weigh up to 800 grams (28 ounces). It initially came in the subdued shades of the Highlands: browns and pale greens, blues, greys and shades of heather that blended into the terrain like an early form of camouflage. Old tweed even has a characteristic smell created by the lichen dyes, known as crottle, used to create its characteristic flecks.

The original fabric was a twill, known in Scotland as tweel. According to a possibly apocryphal story, it was given the name by which it is now known in about 1830 by a London cloth merchant who misread tweel for tweed in a letter from a Scottish weaving company, and assumed the latter was a brand name taken from the Tweed River, which runs through what was then the heart of the textile manufacturing region in the Scottish Borders. The fabric was consequently promoted as tweed and an industry grew out of the demand south of the border. Production reached its peak in the mid-1960s, when the farmer in the field, the gentleman in his club and young lecturers at the new British universities all wore tweed jackets.

Some aspired to the king of tweeds: Harris tweed or *clo mhor* (the big cloth) in Gaelic. A brand name in itself, at one time it encompassed over 8000 different designs (thanks to the introduction of more advanced looms during the 1920s). It is the catch-all term for tweed made with local wool, which is today spun and dyed by machine but still hand-woven by islanders in their homes on the Scottish islands of Harris, Uist, Lewis and Barra in the Outer Hebrides.

Harris tweeds were first put on a commercial footing by Lady Catherine Herbert, the widow of Alexander, 6th Earl of Dunmore and owner of the North Harris estate. In 1846 she commissioned skilled Harris weavers to copy a tartan for jackets worn by the estate's gamekeepers. The detail and colour of the fabric impressed her landed gentry friends, and it became fashionable as far away as Queen Victoria's court circle in London. The cloth, and in particular a tweed suit, came to define what a gentleman wore in the country, and was also central to men's semirural wear.

In 1909 genuine Harris tweed was granted a certification mark that defined it as 'a tweed, hand-spun, hand-woven and dyed by the crofters and cottars in the Outer Hebrides'. This gave it the type of *appellation contrôlée* applied to the likes of champagne and cognac, and was a prescient move: during the 1930s an attempt by weavers on the Scottish mainland to imitate it in order to capitalize on its popularity resulted in a record civil case. Harris tweed won and its provenance was protected. Later legal changes allowed the fabric to be made with wool from anywhere in the world. However, while Harris tweed's fortunes have fluctuated, the old-world appeal of the tweed jacket has not.

Opposite: Jimmy Stewart in relaxed mode in a studio publicity shot. Below: Although different estates in Scotland have had distinctive colours and patterns of tweed, the tonal range of the most typical variants is clearly that of the British countryside: moss, heather, bark.

6.
SHIRTS & SWEATERS

THE SHIRT / THE SWEATSHIRT / THE BUTTON-DOWN SHIRT / THE GUERNSEY SWEATER / THE HAWAIIAN SHIRT / THE POLO SHIRT / THE LUMBERJACK SHIRT / THE BRETON TOP / THE CARDIGAN

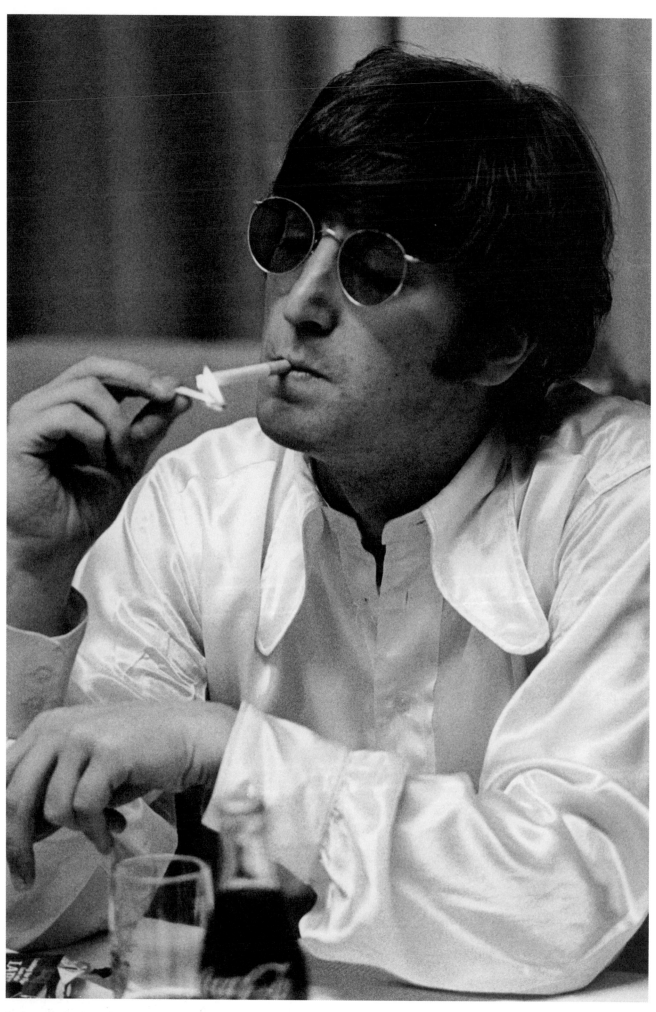

THE SHIRT

SHIRTS & SWEATERS

A stroll down London's Jermyn Street can leave no one in any doubt about the role the classic business shirt plays in the male wardrobe. While other cities, such as Venice, may have a long pedigree in shirtmaking, this single street is the epicentre of the craft. Named after Henry Jermyn (1604–84), 1st Earl of St Albans, who was responsible for much of the development of London's West End as a business and retail Mecca, it was a magnet for elite shirtmakers who, over generations, defined the characteristics of the quality shirt: among them the split yoke and multiple pleats where sleeve meets cuff. By the late nineteenth century few other trades were represented on the street.

Although the shirt became a lynchpin of business dress and later, in its many softer forms, also of casual wear, its beginnings were less auspicious. It started life during the Middle Ages as a form of underwear, the first layer against the skin, which is one reason why white shirts came to be so highly prized: they suggested a man had sufficient status and wealth to be able to wear fresh linen every day, which would have been necessary given the limited hygiene of the times. In fact, wearing a pristine shirt was regarded as an acceptable substitute for bodily cleanliness. So prized were shirts, in linen or silk, that they were given as prestige gifts and were part of wedding dowries.

Until the early twentieth century only the well-to-do changed their shirts regularly. Before then, although the first button-through front shirt was registered by London tailors Brown, Davies & Co. in 1871, a shirt was typically donned by pulling it over the head and was cut long enough to double as a nightshirt. The collarless shirt, the 1827 invention of Hannah Montague, a housewife who was tired of scrubbing a tidemark of dirt from her husband's collar, was widely worn until the 1930s; a fresh collar and cuffs could be fixed to it each day, and its hidden main body, often in bold colours and patterns, was worn repeatedly without being washed. A clean white collar indicated the status of the new aspiring class of office-based employees or 'white-collar workers'.

Opposite: John Lennon, his shirt collar distinctively late 1960s. Below: The shirt provides a gentleman with the opportunity to revel in stripe and pattern in a way few other clothing types do – something London tailor Gieves played on in its brochures.

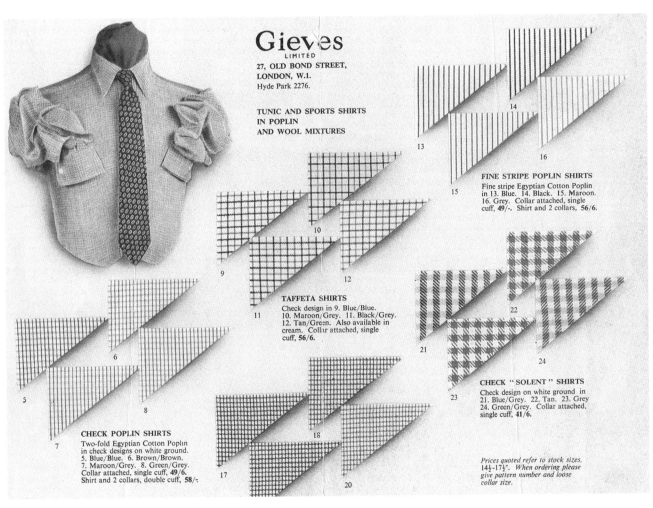

Gieves
LIMITED
27, OLD BOND STREET,
LONDON, W.1.
Hyde Park 2276.

TUNIC AND SPORTS SHIRTS IN POPLIN AND WOOL MIXTURES

FINE STRIPE POPLIN SHIRTS
Fine stripe Egyptian Cotton Poplin in 13. Blue. 14. Black. 15. Maroon. 16. Grey. Collar attached, single cuff, 49/-. Shirt and 2 collars, 56/6.

TAFFETA SHIRTS
Check design in 9. Blue/Blue. 10. Maroon/Grey. 11. Black/Grey. 12. Tan/Green. Also available in cream. Collar attached, single cuff, 56/6.

CHECK "SOLENT" SHIRTS
Check design on white ground in 21. Blue/Grey. 22. Tan. 23. Grey 24. Green/Grey. Collar attached, single cuff, 41/6.

CHECK POPLIN SHIRTS
Two-fold Egyptian Cotton Poplin in check designs on white ground. 5. Blue/Blue. 6. Brown/Brown. 7. Maroon/Grey. 8. Green/Grey. Collar attached, single cuff, 49/6. Shirt and 2 collars, double cuff, 58/-.

Prices quoted refer to stock sizes, 14½-17½". When ordering please give pattern number and loose collar size.

Because the shirt was initially regarded as underwear, emphasis was placed on the collar, the part that was most visible, and its accoutrements, such as cravats and ties. During Europe's Thirty Years War (1618–38), when shorter hairstyles for men came into vogue, the collar ran the gamut of extremes, from the small flat French style through to what Italian courts of the time referred to as the *giorgiera*, which was created with an incredible 11 metres (36 feet) of fabric.

Shirts may not have involved such excesses, but they provided opportunities for personal expression well into the twentieth century: shirtmakers such as Cluett, Peabody & Co. in the United States, the company behind the pioneering Arrow brand of shirts, regularly offered the same shirt body with perhaps 30 variations of turn-down collar style – many more than the spread, club, pin, point, cutaway, tab and button-down varieties now available from specialists.

Indeed, by the twentieth century collar styles were increasingly subject to fashion: in 1900 any self-respecting man about town wore a high-band, a 7.5-centimetre (3-inch) wall of starched rigid linen, capable of bruising the jaw if the wearer turned his head too far. Other changes to the shirt were responses to advances in lifestyle. The first breast pockets, for example, were introduced in the 1960s. When central heating in homes and offices became more widespread the demise of what was then the typical male attire of waistcoat or three-piece suit followed, and a breast pocket became useful. What has lasted is the centrality of the shirt in the modern male wardrobe: stiff-collared, it remains key to received ideas of business attire and smart dress.

Opposite: Brooks Brothers, creators of one of the most distinctive shirt styles: the button-down, shown here in a catalogue page from the 1970s. **Below:** Even a shirt unfastened at the neck, as one may now commonly wear it, was not acceptable for much of the garment's history. Once considered to be underwear, revealing too much of it was taboo – a notion of *déshabillé* that Lord Byron and the Romantic poets played on and which modern dress etiquette recognizes in the insistence that a gentleman keeps his jacket on unless he is invited to remove it.

BROOKSGATE

Brooksgate shirts are made exclusively for us from a pattern with the trimmer lines that many young men prefer. We offer them in collar sizes 14 to 16½, long sleeves 32 to 35.

A. Long sleeve, button-down collar cotton oxford shirt in blue, white, yellow, pink or ecru. H296, **$22** ($2.45).
As above, of polyester-and-cotton in white, blue, pink or yellow. H310, **$21** ($2.45).
Yellow silk foulard neckwear. H479, **$12.50** ($1.85).

B. Candy striped cotton oxford shirt with button-down collar and long sleeves. Wine or blue on white. H309, **$22** ($2.45).
As above, of polyester-and-cotton. H297, **$21** ($2.45).
Wine silk foulard neckwear. H477, **$12.50** ($1.85).

C. Tattersall shirt of cotton-and-polyester has long sleeves and button-down collar. Red-blue or green-blue on white. H386, **$22** ($2.45).
Knit neckwear of wool-and-mohair in yellow, forest green, burgundy, navy, camel or blue mix. H487, **$10** ($1.85).

D. Solid color cotton broadcloth Brooksgate shirts with plain point collar and long sleeves. Blue or white. H393, **$22** ($2.45).
Dark red silk foulard neckwear. H470; or navy, H476. **$12.50** ($1.85).

30

THE SWEAT-SHIRT

SHIRTS & SWEATERS

It is one of the most innocuous garments in the male wardrobe, mass-manufactured like the T-shirt or jeans, but with neither's rock 'n' roll credibility. Yet when Steve McQueen, as the 'cooler king' in *The Great Escape* (1963), wore one under his A2 flight jacket and, later, during his motorcycle escape attempt, the humble sweatshirt attained a touch of cool. Indeed, although the movie is set during the Second World War, it was around the time of its release that the sweatshirt made its transition from being strictly a sports garment to one worn casually. Before collegiate preppy style adopted it, before Virgil Hilts, and long before the 1980s when designer fashion appropriated it, the sweatshirt was merely a solution to a problem.

During the early 1920s sportspeople wore a knitted woollen sweater, typically grey, in order to keep warm before and after training. Inevitably it needed regular washing but was prone to shrinkage and slow to dry. By the end of the decade this had changed. The first example of what is now regarded as a sweatshirt – a simple, loose, collarless pullover made of soft, thick woven cotton (then still grey) – was produced by Russell, a company founded by Benjamin Russell in Alexander City, Alabama, in 1902 to make women's and children's underwear. Business was solid but a new generation's thinking inspired new products: in about 1922 Benjamin's son Bennie, a keen American football player while he was at the University of Alabama, suggested that the company's women's union-suit top should be modified to create shirts for him and his teammates.

Until this time football uniforms were heavy woollen garments, impractical and, typically worn next to the skin, uncomfortable. The new product – plain, unremarkable but familiar and, like jeans, khakis and leather jackets, better-looking with age – was a huge hit, even though an anonymous Russell employee named it, however accurately, the sweatshirt. Russell shipped the first batch to its Philadelphia distributor, who sent the garments to four local football teams. They sold out immediately. Sales to baseball as well as football players, and to athletes, followed and the sweatshirt became ubiquitous among sportspeople,

Opposite: Actor, and future president of the United States, Ronald Reagan, in athletic mode. **Right**: American man of letters John Steinbeck at his home in Sag Harbor, Long Island.

professional and amateur alike. Within a decade Russell had created a new division, Russell Athletic, solely to handle the new sweatshirt business – which ultimately replaced the underwear lines.

A second development in the creation of the sweatshirt increased its potential. In 1919 brothers Abe and Bill Feinbloom established the Knickerbocker Knitting Company – trading under the name Champion – and shortly after patented a flocking process that enabled raised lettering to be printed on fabric. The weight and thickness of the sweatshirt fabric made it the ideal site for such printing. By the early 1930s the sweatshirt was no longer just a functional item, but one that indicated membership of a high-school team, showed allegiance to it, promoted a company or displayed a slogan.

Champion was quick to see how sweatshirt fabric could be used for other sporting clothing. It was first to create an outsize, zip-up, hooded sweatshirt, originally worn by football players over their uniforms and padding when they were on the sidelines. The company also developed the first reverse-weave sweatshirt; the light ribbing ran horizontally across the body rather than vertically up it, which meant minor shrinkages did not affect its length, no matter how many times the sweaty garment was washed. The machine on which these sweatshirts were made was known as a loopwheel. It was slow and inefficient by modern manufacturing standards, but minimized any tension when the thread was being woven and arguably created a better garment. Loopwheel machines fell out of wide use during the 1950s, but the garments they produced are much sought after by clothing collectors.

Opposite: Buster Keaton in characteristically playful mood in *Sidewalks of New York* (1931). **Below:** Members of the American gold-winning rowing eight at the Berlin Olympics of 1936. Dominating the sports apparel market for sweatshirts were Russell Athletic and Champion, the latter creator of both a flocking process that allowed lettering to be printed on to fabric, as in the pictures here, and also the reverse-weave sweatshirt, which ensured that no lengthways shrinkage occurred.

THE BUTTON-DOWN SHIRT

SHIRTS & SWEATERS

Menswear has a habit of taking sartorial ideas out of context and making them work. The button-down shirt is an example of one such transition. It began on an English polo field in 1896, where one of the spectators was John Brooks, grandson of the founder of Brooks Brothers – arguably the most famous and influential name in American men's clothing. Polo players then adhered to strict rules of propriety in dress and rode in formal shirts, with one important modification: buttons were attached to keep the collar affixed to the shirt's main body and prevent it flapping into the rider's face.

It was a workaday style. And one, Brooks saw, with potential. The Brooks Brothers button-down shirt was initially made from whitish Oxford cloth, soon after in pink and later in many colours and stripes, and came to be a new American symbol of youth and vitality. It was a huge success from the moment it went on sale in about 1900, as 'the original polo shirt', and remains a best-selling item. Its introduction not only brought a more casual element to men's dressing, it also changed the nature of shirts in the United States. Until this time they were collarless and worn with separate, stiff, attachable collars that could be easily detached and washed.

The button-down was more comfortable, more bohemian and almost avant-garde, and by 1915, along with Brooks Brothers Number One sack suit, was part of wealthy collegiate life, especially at America's East Coast educational institutions Harvard and Yale. Winthrop Brooks, president of Brooks Brothers from 1935 to 1946 and an heir to the business, was a member of the Whiffenpoofs, Yale's singing society, which was typically kitted out in head-to-toe Brooks Brothers. F. Scott Fitzgerald wore the shirt at a time when it was still considered a daring choice.

By the years just before the Second World War the button-down, along with collegiate sweatshirts, cardigans, loafers and khakis, was an essential part of the smart-but-relaxed preppy uniform of students and men about town. It also suggested something of the upper crust: in John O'Hara's novels, for example, among them *Appointment in Samarra*, the baddies invariably wore loud clothes and the good guys – typically well-to-do – wore Brooks, including the neat button-down. The shirt also came to represent a certain conservatism: in Mary McCarthy's short story 'The Man in the Brooks Brothers Shirt', clothes symbolize the ambitions of a straitened steel industry executive – in a button-down shirt – and are contrasted with those worn by the more artistic love interest.

What perhaps sealed the shirt's status as a menswear icon was celebrity. Clark Gable, Hollywood superstar, may have killed the vest – after he took his shirt off to reveal a bare chest in *It Happened One Night* (1934), sales of vests plummeted – but he helped make the button-down shirt. With his 112-centimetre (44-inch) chest and 81-centimetre (32-inch) waist, he was generally ill-suited to most ready-to-wear-clothing of the time – with the exception of the Brooks Brothers button-down shirt. He became a lifetime fan and a source of promotion that money could not buy. Tyrone Power subsequently wore the shirt in *The Razor's Edge* (1946), Fred Astaire in *Funny Face* (1957) and Cary Grant in *North by Northwest* (1959).

As in the movies, so in industry and art. Fiat supremo Gianni Agnelli popularized the style in Europe and wore his favourite blue, white or ecru button-downs with characteristic style: watch strapped over the cuff and collar buttons undone. Andy Warhol wore the shirt in white only.

Opposite: F. Scott Fitzgerald wearing a Brooks Brothers button-down shirt. The style was initially made in an off-white Oxford cloth called karnak, after the Egyptian city where linen of the same colour was found in ancient tombs. Brooks Brothers found its Oxford cloth at a Scottish manufacturer, D. & J. Anderson, in 1875. The button-down was also the original polo shirt, worn by polo players until it was replaced by the soft-collared sports style pioneered by René Lacoste that is now more commonly known by his surname.

ポロカラーシャツ

一般には〝ボタンダウンシャツ〟の名で親しまれているこのシャツは、1900年、元社長ジョン・ブルックスが、英国で観戦したポロ競技の選手が着ていたシャツにヒントを得て、世界で初めて考案したものである。

'Now I wear a gansey and around me waist a belt / I'm the gaffer of the squads that makes the hot asphalt' as the lyric of the Gaelic folk song 'Hot Asphalt' has it. But the Guernsey sweater was always more seafarer's than labourer's garb. Fishermen traditionally had two Guernseys: one for work, which was rarely washed and was embedded with protective oils, the other for church on Sundays. The sweater is knitted flat so that it can be worn either way round, allowing it to be thrown on at a moment's notice and still be comfortable; it can also be turned round if certain areas, such as the elbows, are in need of repair.

THE GUERNSEY SWEATER

SHIRTS & SWEATERS

The Guernsey sweater may be the oldest unchanged garment in the male wardrobe. It dates back to the sixteenth century and the reign of Elizabeth I when, for the first time, English seafaring was on an oceanic scale and trade grew internationally. The need for seamen to be protected from the elements resulted in a sweater designed specifically for them, which was developed in the cottage industry of Guernsey, one of Britain's Channel Islands, and in other rugged coastal communities. So entrenched was the sweater as part of the seafaring image, and so successful the design, that some two centuries later Horatio Nelson, admiral of the English fleet, ordered that the style be issued to crews serving in the Royal Navy.

The Guernsey sweater is also known as a gansey, a now defunct dialect word for the island, and in Gaelic cultures this name is also used for a home-knitted, workmanlike sweater. But the Guernsey is not just any gansey. It is a distinctive item that is traditionally cut to be long and fitted, to provide maximum warmth; it is tightly knitted with five-ply, heavyweight oiled wool – known colloquially as seaman's iron – to give a degree of protection even against rain. A straight, slightly raised collar, higher than a crew neck, is also characteristic, as are the sleeves, which are slightly short of the wrist to keep them dry during work, and to prevent them being caught in equipment.

The sweater is flat and tubular with no side seams, and the pattern, if any, is identical front and back, so a Guernsey can be worn either way round. Unlike most sweaters, it is knitted from the top down; the stitch allows for the arms or lower body to be unravelled and replaced. Vintage Guernseys may show that several complementary but not identical shades of wool have been used over the years.

Although classic Guernsey sweaters are plain, when patterns are incorporated these have a function, not least of which is providing added insulation. Most of them have seafaring connections, be they references to ropes, ladders, anchors, nets, herring bones, the waves or the elements, and in the past were badges of belonging to specific fishing communities. Small, personal variations in a pattern, or the subtle incorporation of initials, could be used to identify a specific member of a crew if he fell overboard and drowned and the body was not recovered for some time. There are also symbolic patterns, such as the zigzag 'marriage lines' typical to Filey, on England's north-eastern coast, which are said to reflect the good times and bad in a relationship.

Fishing communities in the United Kingdom are more remote than communities further inland and, despite the gradual industrialization of knitting, a degree of self-sufficiency was inevitable. Guernsey sweaters continued to be widely made domestically well into the twentieth century, as a matter of community pride. Patterns, memorized rather than written down, were passed from mother to daughter, and each generation added its tweaks. Each hand-knitted sweater became a work of local art or craft, and remains a piece of menswear history – and essential gear for any sea dog worth his sea salt.

THE HAWAIIAN SHIRT

SHIRTS & SWEATERS

The Hawaiian shirt is the clown of the male wardrobe. If men have largely been constrained to straight lines and sober colours since Georgian times, this outlandish garment remains a last bastion of colour, pattern and excess. For brands such as Kahala, which has become the exemplar of the contemporary style, it is a kind of canvas, and the shirts are as appealing framed as worn. The best older pieces are masterworks of detail, from the hand-printing in up to 20 colours, and the matched pockets and longer collars of the earlier styles, to buttons traditionally carved from native coconut (20 buttons to a nut). The shirts, which date to the 1920s, were also at the forefront of fabric innovation – the most highly prized are 'silkies' made from cool spun rayon or, after 1953, from Dacron, an early version of polyester.

For some people the shirt is a wearable postcard, for others an expression of positivity. For the people of Hawaii they are a point of cultural pride. Few items of men's clothing, with perhaps the exception of the Stetson and the Nehru collar, have come to be so firmly associated with one place: the Hawaiian shirt, sometimes called the Aloha Shirt, is the worldwide symbol of the United States' 50th state.

By the 1930s it had become synonymous with vacationing and was worn by every holidaying film star from John Barrymore to Al Jolson, Douglas Fairbanks to Ronald Colman. With hat and pipe, the shirt came to define Bing Crosby's look (especially in the road movies he made with Bob Hope). It was a favourite of rat-packer Peter Lawford, and Montgomery Clift got his come-uppance wearing one in *From Here to Eternity* (1953). Presidents Eisenhower and Truman wore Hawaiian shirts at weekends.

The origins of the shirt remain a mystery. Some say the first one was made by a Japanese tailor in Hawaii from kimono cloth, others that it derives from the so-called tails-out shirts native to the Philippines, yet others that it migrated from Tahiti, where images of hibiscus, breadfruit and other exotica have long been

Opposite: Tom Selleck in *Magnum P.I.* (1980-88), driver of a Ferrari Testarossa, bearer of a moustache and, true to his island beat, wearer of Hawaiian shirts. Their earliest recorded reference was made some 60 years earlier, in 1927, when a Gordon Young created a ruckus by wearing one to the University of Washington. **Below and right:** © 1956–2009 Tori Richard, Ltd. All rights reserved.

printed on cloth. The western shirt was introduced to Hawaii by Captain Cook in the late eighteenth century (somewhat tight-fistedly, as it was exchanged for a prized royal cloak from King Kalaniopuu). Missionaries subsequently taught the islanders how to sew so that they could cover up their offensive nakedness. And, finally, Chinese and Japanese brought to Hawaii to work on pineapple and sugar plantations introduced not only their own printed silks and traditional fabrics, but also the art of tailoring. In short, history conspired to put a bright turquoise-and-banana-print garment on Elvis's back for *Blue Hawaii* (1961) some 150 years later.

The Hawaiian shirt – a term coined by Ellery J. Chun, a tailor and dry-goods businessman who made it up in 1927 to boost sales, with Aloha Shirt registered nine years later – has enjoyed an uninterrupted pre-eminence in Hawaii's cultural history ever since it first dazzled US naval crews and Hollywood big shots in the 1930s. Such was the shirt's appeal, to both natives and visitors, that within a decade Honolulu had 275 tailors and the great Hawaiian shirt labels had been born: Royal Hawaiian Manufacturing Co., Haw Togs, Holo-Holo, Malihiwi Sportswear and the Kamehemeha Garment Co. among them.

By 1947 employees of Hawaii's city councils were allowed to wear Hawaiian shirts to work and in 1948 Aloha Wednesday, a precursor to dress-down Friday, was introduced across the islands. Duke Kahanamoku – founding father of surfing and Hawaii's most famous son – was brought in to promote Hawaiian shirts. By 1958 their manufacture was the islands' third biggest industry, with many of their inhabitants hard at work making them. They did not take the advice of Duke Kahanamoku, printed in an early 1950s advertisement for the shirt: 'Hoomanau Nui' (Take it Easy).

Opposite and right: Shirts by Tori Richard, Honolulu. One of Hawaii's big names in big-print shirts since 1956, its styles include both traditional patterns inspired by nature and island life and more geometric, contemporary designs. The clothes of Hawaii's earliest inhabitants were also characteristically bold; barkwood cloths were stained with the juice of kukui nuts to create red and yellow ochre shades. © 1956–2009 Tori Richard, Ltd. All rights reserved.

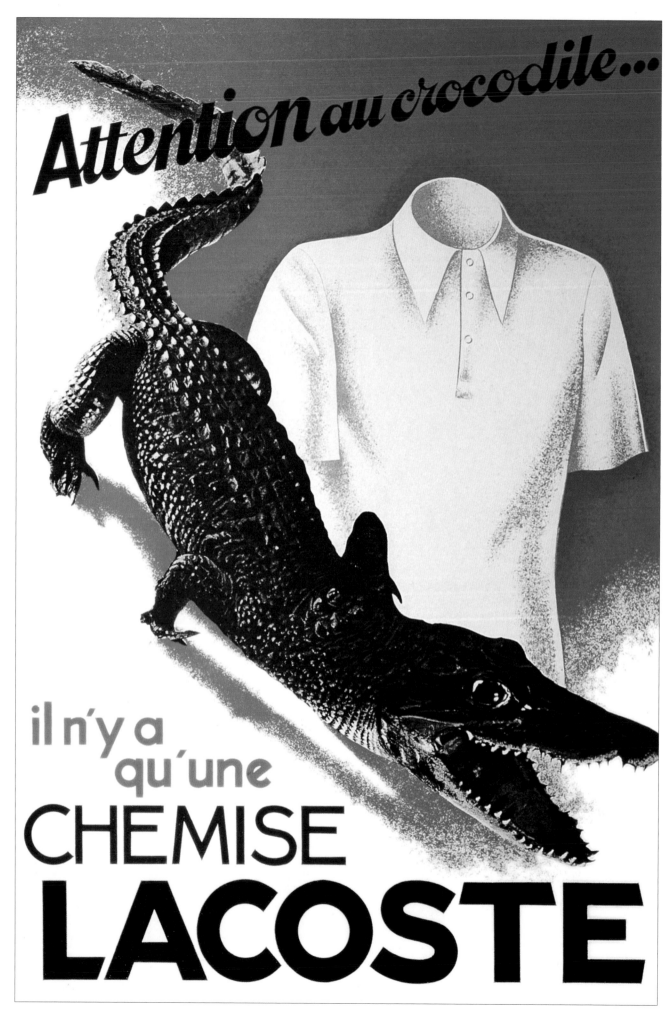

THE POLO SHIRT

SHIRTS & SWEATERS

It began with a wager to encourage the captain of the French Davis Cup squad to lead his team to victory – the prize for winning was a set of alligator-skin luggage – and ended with one of the most counterfeited logos in menswear: a small alligator. The logo would overshadow the sporting triumphs of the man behind it, René Lacoste, winner of seven Grand Slam titles. And it would overshadow his contributions to tennis racquet design, including the first steel racquet and the first shock dampener. Indeed, the logo – designed by the artist Robert George after 'the alligator' became a nickname for the tennis ace – has become better known than all it emblazons, with the exception of perhaps one item: the piqué polo shirt.

Before Lacoste, professional tennis was a sport of rigorous sartorial rules: women dressed in blouses and full-length skirts; men in flannel trousers and full-sleeved shirts, sleeves rolled. Until, that is, Lacoste wore a short-sleeved shirt in a lightweight, breathable cotton known as jersey petit piqué, with an unstarched collar – soft but stiff enough to be turned up to protect the back of the neck from the sun – and three-button placket. Originally, styles had a longer cut at the rear, known as the tennis tail, to prevent the shirt coming out of the trousers into which it was tucked.

The polo shirt – as it came to be more commonly known after it was adopted by polo players, who had also been constrained by heavy shirts – debuted at the 1927 United States men's championship. How much of Lacoste's success on court can be attributed to his ground-breaking clothing is debatable, but the polo shirt's ease of wear off court prompted him to create a business. He joined forces with knitwear manufacturing entrepreneur Andre Gillier in 1933 and the shirt, known as the 12-12, went into commercial production. Initially produced only in white, it is now available in the full spectrum of colours.

As happens with many menswear icons derived from sports clothes, the practicality of the design soon saw the polo shirt being worn away from the tennis court or field of play. Because of its collar, it has been deemed a more

Right: René Lacoste, co-creator of the polo shirt. Initially the style was available only in white, as befitted – despite its name – its designed purpose as a shirt for tennis.

Left and below: DJ Norman Jaye (below) and musician Paul Weller (bottom left), here at the time of fronting The Jam, demonstrate the correct way to wear the polo shirt – buttoned to the neck and collar turned down (unlike the WASPish variant of collar turned up). Contrary to public image the uniform of the skinhead subculture (bottom) was one of immense sartorial detail.

formal alternative to the T-shirt. It has crossed social boundaries, and over the decades has come to represent distinct social classes, be they Euro hiphop kids in the *banlieue* of Paris, British mods, American West Coast skaters or the wealthy preppy set of Long Island, New York.

Other brands followed Lacoste with their own take on the polo shirt and have won loyal followings. British-born Fred Perry hailed from the same sporting background as Lacoste, and was an eight-time winner of Grand Slam titles and the World No.1 player for five years. After his retirement in the late 1940s he was approached by Austrian footballer-turned-entrepreneur Tibby Wegner, who had an idea for an antiperspirant device to be worn on the wrist; a few modifications by Perry resulted in the sweatband. Wegner also suggested a branded polo shirt with Perry's victory laurel logo, loosely based on an old Wimbledon Championship one. Also initially available only in white, it was launched at Wimbledon in 1952. It was a mod staple by the end of the decade, and later a key element of skinhead and northern soul uniforms.

More recently, Ralph Lauren developed his Polo brand. With its embroidered polo-player logo, it references the rich man's equestrian sport more than tennis and, in doing so, makes the polo shirt totemic of a well-to-do WASPish lifestyle.

Above: The big polo match: Lacoste vs. Perry. On the right is Perry himself in action.

THE LUMBER-JACK SHIRT

SHIRTS & SWEATERS

In 1963 The Majorettes released 'White Levi's, Tennis Shoes, Surfin' Hat and Big Plaid Pendleton Shirt', which, aside from being a good example of girl group as effective stylists, reflected the extent to which the Pendleton shirt had become ingrained in American culture. The single went to number one.

The early 1960s also saw The Pendletones, whose look – a winter-weight Pendleton worn jacket-style, open over a white T-shirt, with jeans – created a new college campus uniform. In time the group became associated with the Hawaiian shirt and better known as The Beach Boys. There is not much call for woollen shirts in California, but surfers of the period sometimes used a plaid shirt as a quick cover-up when they left the waves, and the garment came to be nicknamed a 'board shirt'.

The Pendleton continued to have resonance for the music industry with the advent of grunge in the 1990s, which, like the shirt, grew out of the American Northwest (notably Seattle). Much the same youth uniform, albeit taking a grubbier, more distressed, anti-fashion, thrift-store form, reflected a darker, countercultural music.

While Pendleton is the benchmark in woollen work shirts, these were established before the brand was launched in the first decade of the twentieth century. But early shirts were functional products, plain and mostly grey. Bold plaid patterns, now associated with the archetypal blue-collar working man – construction worker or, more frontiersman, the lumberjack – were Pendleton's contribution. Worn over a red flannel undershirt, its shirt sets the rugged, manly style for work in the great outdoors, and clothing to relax in come the weekend.

Although the shirt is quintessentially American, the Pendleton company owes its origins to an immigrant, one Thomas Kay from England. In 1863 he travelled to the new American state of Oregon to join its burgeoning wool-milling industry and, in 1889, set up his own mill in Salem, Massachusetts. In 1909, his grandsons Clarence, Chauncey and Roy acquired a mill in Pendleton, Oregon,

Opposite: Rock Hudson, but not his usual clean-cut self, in a lumberjack shirt. **Below:** The Pendletones, named after their Pendleton-shirt uniform and soon to rename themselves The Beach Boys.

that had fallen on hard times when a venture to supply bed blankets for Native Americans failed. The Bishops relaunched the business, and by responding to the local preference for stronger colours and jacquard patterns, rather than the dour plaids and block-colour designs that had been offered, made a success of it. They were soon selling blankets that had ceremonial significance as well as trade value to Native American nations far and wide.

Three years later they took their first step towards the lumberjack shirt when they established a new mill to make softer fabrics, including virgin wool. Their intention was to apply the same design philosophy to warm but drab men's work shirts as they had applied to the blankets. It was some time before the idea was realized, but in 1924 the first Pendleton virgin wool plaid shirt came off the production line; light, warm and colourful, it was soon a big hit, even purely as a fashion. 'Another winter mode that is spreading like wildfire is the lumberjack shirt,' wrote a correspondent for the metropolitan American trade journal *Men's Fashions* in early 1925. 'It is, however, only modelled after lumberjack shirts, as the real ones sold in the north country are extremely heavy…'.

Within five years Pendleton was producing a full line of men's sportswear. The woollen shirt became so central to the concept of winter dressing for men that it was 1972 before the company first launched clothing for summer. It remains a family business, with many of its shirts still made by hand in order to ensure the careful matching of their highly patterned components.

Opposite: Pendleton's early advertising played on the lumberjack shirt's associations with the great outdoors, even if the only activity involved was raking the lawn. Pendleton was at least founded in the great outdoors, in Oregon – the conditions there were ideal for sheep rearing and its soft waters were perfect for wool production. **Right:** More recent advertising aims to capture the same mood of masculinity.

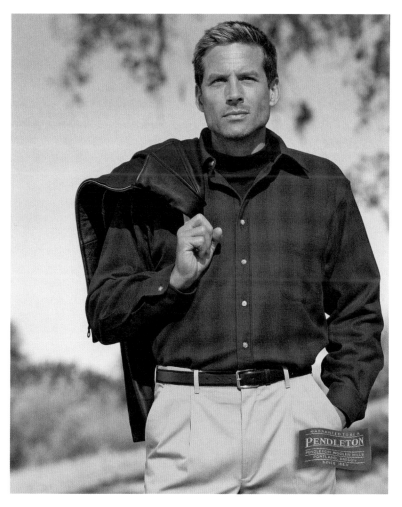

THE BRETON TOP

SHIRTS & SWEATERS

Opposite: Marion Mitchell Morrison, better known as John Wayne, 'the Duke', in seafaring mode for *Reap the Wild Wind* (1942), rather than his usual cowboy style.

A type of clothing can speak of a certain era or suggest a certain person. But few garments still widely worn today encapsulate a particular nation – and, indeed, shape public perception, however stereotyped, of how its inhabitants dress. But just as lederhosen are undeniably German and the bowler hat is English, the Breton top is as French as Camembert, even if it was the signature choice of the likes of James Dean and Kurt Cobain, Andy Warhol and, most famously, Pablo Picasso, none of whom was French.

At least two famed Frenchmen, Jean-Paul Gaultier and Jean-Paul Sartre, have also favoured it. The former used it to play on the idea of Frenchness for photographers Pierre et Gilles (then made it his signature); the latter helped the Breton top become associated with postwar, countercultural and existential angst as much as it was perceived as a traditional, or nearly national, kind of dress. When costume designer Edith Head envisaged Cary Grant's French Resistance leader turned suave cat burglar in Alfred Hitchcock's *To Catch a Thief* (1955) she dressed him in a Breton top.

Gabrielle 'Coco' Chanel, who appropriated much sportswear and workwear from the male wardrobe, had made the simple blue and white-striped, boat-necked, knitted shirt famous nearly three decades previously as a womenswear item. She is said to have been inspired by seeing fishermen at work while on holiday at Deauville on the French coast; in turn, the likes of Jean Seberg and Audrey Hepburn made the style their own. But the shirt, for all its occasionally fey leanings, could hardly be more masculine. The *marinière*, as the French call it, was created by an act of the French government on 27 March 1858 as part of the official uniform of the French navy. The Russian navy also adopted the look.

Fishermen in the Brittany region of north-western France had long worn warm, loose-fitting versions of the top, with three-quarter length sleeves and, according to France's Musée de la Marine, specifically 22 blue and white stripes – in part out of regional pride, and in part because the stripes made it easier to see anyone who fell overboard. The Breton top was not the only practical item of naval dress that was eventually assimilated by fashion and adopted as chic rather than, as with much army clothing, subversive: others included the sailor top (a lightweight blue canvas V-neck pullover), bell-bottom trousers (which could easily be rolled up when swabbing the deck), knotted neckerchief, espadrilles and the naval cap.

The shirt's first transformation from working to fashion item was not entirely welcomed. In 1934 *Adam*, a style-watching magazine of the interwar period, noted that the French Riviera was being overrun by bohemian young men wearing a 'fashionable sailor outfit' of Breton top and (that other French clothing icon) beret. 'We urgently ask our friends to see that all grotesque individuals of this type vanish immediately,' its commentator requested. The second wave of appreciation of the shirt, amid the burgeoning youth culture of Paris after the Second World War (and prefiguring beat culture in the United States), made the Breton similar to a French take on the all-American plain white T-shirt. If the white T was the choice of Marlon Brando's Johnny in *The Wild One* (1953), Lee Marvin, playing his fellow rebel biker, wore something akin to a Breton, in blue and yellow.

THE CARDIGAN

SHIRTS & SWEATERS

Many clothing types have won a kind of immortality for individuals who were honoured or celebrated during their lives: the Chesterfield coat, or perhaps the Windsor knotted tie. But the cardigan commemorates a man who is associated with a military disaster. James Thomas Brudenell (1797–1868) was a British army officer who was beset with scandal throughout his life: he was removed from a military post for misconduct and later tried by the House of Lords for fighting a duel. He was serving in the Crimean War in 1854 when, as a result of a series of miscommunications, he was ordered to lead a suicidal cavalry charge against Russian cannon. Many of his men were killed, and their courage was remembered in Alfred, Lord Tennyson's poem 'The Charge of the Light Brigade'.

Brudenell was also the 7th Earl of Cardigan and, in part because the cavalry charge had made him famous, his soft, thick, fur-trimmed and braided button-through sweater – which he is said to have worn because he could slip it on and off without disarranging his hair – became a fashion craze in high society, even though it was derived from traditional fishermen's clothing that dated to the seventeenth century. The cardigan, as it became known, was not the only garment to come out of the Crimean War: the balaclava, a woollen accessory that covered the entire head, was named after the town, now in the Ukraine, near where the Light Brigade's charge took place. But while balaclavas have something of a reputation for being worn by sinister characters, the cardigan's origins in warfare could hardly be further from its more modern associations: fireside and grandfatherly attire.

The cardigan's association with an older generation was perhaps most vividly demonstrated when David Bowie and Bing Crosby teamed up for a Christmas television performance of 'Little Drummer Boy' in 1977. The former wore a sharp jacket, denims and turn-ups, the latter was in an open-neck shirt and grey Slazenger cardigan, albeit without his trademark pipe. But this belies the cardigan's potential to have a much edgier image; James 'Gene' Tunney, the heavyweight boxing champion of 1926–28 made the shawl-collar version a macho trademark out of the ring, and during the early 1990s Nirvana's Kurt Cobain reinvented the cardigan's appeal through grunge.

During the years after the Second World War the menswear industry slowly began to distinguish between a man's working wardrobe and what he wore for leisure. Cardigans were considered inappropriate for the workplace, and thus became symbolic of relaxation; they were particularly popular in the avant-garde beat scene of the American West Coast and with the intelligentsia of the Parisian Left Bank. Heavy-knit, zip-up and/or shawl-collar styles became popular country sportswear.

Crosby was not the only singing superstar of the era to don the cardigan. The likes of Frank Sinatra and Perry Como were also fans, and their high-rating television shows helped to make the garment fashionable. All three men shared a love of golf, and the cardigan attained a certain swinger credibility through the sport: golf legends Jack Nicklaus, Arnold Palmer and Dan Sanders wore what were known as alpacas – baggy-sleeved, loose-fitting cardigans. Sinatra's annual bill at the store of the Canyon Club in Palm Springs, his local course, was said to run to $30,000 for his knitwear alone. The Voice preferred his cardigans in orange.

The cardigan's appeal also became more youthful during the 1940s and 1950s, thanks to the popularity of the letterman system on American college campuses: students who reached a certain standard in their studies or achieved success in a team sport or performing art were awarded a chenille letter, typically the school's initial. This was generally stitched on to the left breast of a heavy cardigan like those worn by Ritchie Cunningham and Potsie, characters in the 1950s-period television series *Happy Days*; it was also stitched on to a so-called letterman jacket – a crew-neck, baseball-jacket style with a boiled wool body and leather sleeves. Cardigans and jackets alike were prized mementos after graduation.

Opposite: Warren Beatty photographed in 1962. **Below:** Jack Nicholson in a cardigan for one of his first movie roles, *Studs Lonigan* (1960).

7.
ACCESSORIES

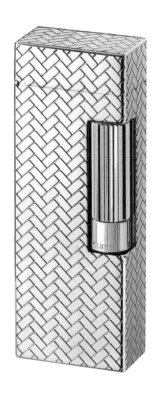

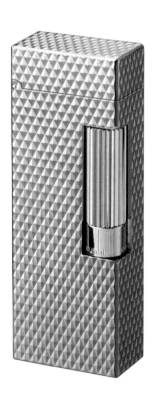

THE LUXURY LIGHTER

ACCESSORIES

The distinctive mechanism may say Dunhill, but the simple design has allowed the Rollagas model to come in many variations, including one that claimed the Guinness record for the world's most expensive lighter. Elvis had a Rollagas in 14-carat gold.

The Dunhill Rollagas lighter became an icon not, like the Zippo, for its functionality, nor even for its sleek lines, but because it epitomized a certain upmarket chic. Just as smoking embodied glamour before the impact of related diseases was understood, so, too, did the Rollagas. Lighting a cigarette with a match may have been part of the act of seduction, but the classy lighter suggested the kind of man who took details of dress seriously, down to how he lit his cigarette.

The Rollagas was also an engineering success. Dunhill, originally a tobacconist and latterly a gentleman's style brand, designed its first experimental gas lighter in 1952, when the company's Swiss manufacturer created a fuel system run on butane, which superseded the petrol-operated Dunhill Auto-Rollalite. Initial problems with the technology meant it was 1955 before the first orders were placed.

The Rollagas was launched – in smoker's paradise Paris – the following year. Import restrictions in France, which limited the number of precious metal items the country could import, only increased the demand for the lighter. In London, where no such restrictions applied, it was offered in every possible finish, including sterling silver and 9-carat gold, and engine-turned and lacquered finishes; a smoker could place on a table a model unlikely to be seen elsewhere. By 1972 a Rollagas in 18-carat gold with a fringe of 200 diamonds claimed the Guiness record as the world's most expensive pocket lighter (cost: £2,750, about £26,000 or $50,000 in 2007). It was a record that Dunhill did not let go lightly. In 1975 it produced a version with 157 diamonds that sold for £4500, while in 1976 a table-top lighter that incorporated the Rollagas was on offer for £32,500.

Such figures guaranteed a high profile for the lighter. But a higher one had already been established: Donald Campbell was given a silver-plate Rollagas to commemorate his breaking the land speed record at Lake Eyre salt flats in Australia on 17 July 1964. In 1967 Colonel Tom Parker, Elvis Presley's manager, gave the singer a 14-carat gold Rollagas; it was subsequently carried around by Presley's bodyguard as the King's trousers were too tight. Anecdotally, during the 1970s a submarine commander lost his lighter and found it a month later wedged into part of the conning tower; despite its prolonged submersion at depth, it is said to have worked the first time he used it again.

Although there were various changes in ornamentation, the Rollagas's design barely altered from the time it was launched, with two exceptions. In 1971, the knuckle hinge on the flip-top was replaced with an integrated hinge. And in 2006 the flame-adjuster was moved from the side of the lighter to the base, so that it no longer caught on clothing, and a separate internal tank was created to make repairs easier (until this time the case itself doubled as the tank). Both exterior advances gave the Rollagas a more streamlined appearance and also placed greater visual emphasis on its most distinctive characteristic: the thumb-operated roll-bar mechanism that produced the flame. As with the Zippo, the sound of the lighter's lid being closed provides part of its appeal, to the extent that proposed updates have been rejected because they would alter the distinctive 'clunk'.

THE PANAMA HAT

ACCESSORIES

Long a favourite of ageing golf pros, dapper horse-racing pundits and the retired middle class, the Panama hat is the king of summer headwear – and perhaps the only icon of menswear to hail from Ecuador. The modern incarnation has been a staple of men's dressing since the early twentieth century and, indeed, was a key accessory during menswear's golden age, from the 1930s through to the early 1950s. The Panama was favoured by movie stars, among them Humphrey Bogart and Gary Cooper, world leaders including Winston Churchill and Harry Truman, and the diverse likes of Salvador Dalí and Frank Sinatra. But the hat's history dates back many centuries.

The Incas clearly knew about keeping cool as well as human sacrifice – in the sixteenth century they were the first to wear Panama-style hats. Called *paja toquilla*, these screened them from the intense sun and were made out of palm leaves. Then, as now, the leaves were stripped into strands not much thicker than thread and woven so tightly – at anything up to 1200 weaves per square 2.5 centimetres (1 inch) – that the result looked like linen.

Each hat is handmade – no two are alike – and takes months of work by one of a dying band of artisans, who prefer to weave without bright light and ideally on a cloudy day as this makes it easier to see the fibres. On the very best examples, the edges are woven back into the brim; on lesser versions the brims are trimmed and sewn. After the hat is made it is pummelled – a craft in itself – to create regularity and suppleness, washed in rainwater, hand-ironed to bring it back to shape and, finally, trimmed. Panamas are naturally pale cream, though darker fibres are sometimes worked into the design for interest's sake, or an entire hat is bleached white using sulphur from the region's volcanoes. The first style that would now be recognizable as a Panama was created by Francisco Delgado in the early eighteenth century. The best examples today – such as those from Hawaiian-based Brent Black or from the London hatmaker Lock & Co., which has sold the hats since 1676 – are still made in Ecuador in the manner effectively laid down by Delgado. Lock was one of the first hatters to help popularize the

Opposite: Mick Jagger of The Rolling Stones in the mid-1970s, with Panama hat, saddle shoes and wide-legged trousers – a rock 'n' roll version of Great Gatsby style.

Making a Panama hat by hand is a long, exhaustive and age-old process. True fans of this headwear accept no imitations.

Panama in Europe; the classic style is most favoured. With a wide brim and black band, it's made in cottage industries in the Ecuadorean provinces of Manabi and Guayas, and focused on the coastal town of Montecristi.

The Panama should technically be known as the Ecuador hat, as it has never been made in Panama. The style received its name when it became internationally known thanks to workers building the Panama shipping canal in the early twentieth century, who donned the hat as protection against the sun. Soon after this, Azuay and Canar, Ecuador's chief hat-production regions, established a vibrant export business – the plants used to make the hats even came to be known as panama hat palms. Royal patronage in England, at a time when royalty was a touchstone for stylish dressing, ensured that the Panama hat became a summer staple.

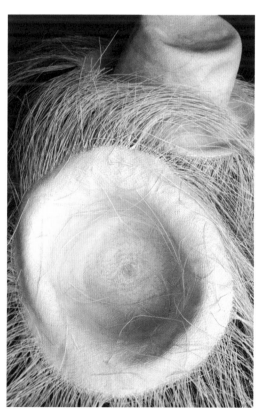

THE FOUNTAIN PEN

ACCESSORIES

It was not the first fountain pen and there are others that have some claim to fame: Waterman's Pink nib, Parker's Duofold, the Pelikan 100, Sheaffer's Lifetime Balance… But, through the cachet it has attained, perhaps no single 'writing instrument' has better helped to maintain the use of fountain pens in the digital age than the Montblanc Meisterstück (Masterpiece) 149.

Its symbolic weight is such that the Department of Foreign Affairs in Berlin (Montblanc was originally a German company) keeps two Meisterstücks on standby for the signing of treaties. It is the pen most frequently used to complete other important agreements, from business deals to registering a marriage; John F. Kennedy signed-off laws with one and Ernest Hemingway wrote notes with his.

While writing with the 149 is substantially no different to using any other prestige pen, it has become the design classic, on permanent display in the Museum of Modern Art, New York. In 1974 Roger Moore, appearing as James Bond, used a gold Meisterstück – adapted by gadget boffin Q – to shoot the eponymous hitman in *The Man with the Golden Gun* (1974). He used another in *Octopussy* (1983).

The pen was launched in 1924, the 149 simply an internal production number. But the 4810 hand-engraved on the nib was more significant, as it is the height in metres of Mont Blanc, Europe's highest mountain. Two other marks identified the chunky but plain black barrel as being that of a Meisterstück: three gold or platinum rings and a white six-pointed 'star' at the tip of the cap, a reference to the six glaciers around Mont Blanc's peak. This subtle if conspicuous piece of branding helped the Meisterstück to become a sometimes showy benchmark of good taste.

By the time the Meisterstück was launched the company behind it was well established. The Hamburg-based stationer Claus-Johannes Voss, the engineer August Eberstein and the salesman Alfred Nehemias met in 1906 to exchange business ideas. They decided to take on the then fledgling fountain pen market that was slowly growing in England and the United States, with Waterman the leader in the American market.

Voss had the greatest insight: that a fountain pen with an ink container independent of an inkwell would be the perfect product for an increasingly dynamic and mobile society. The three men established the Simplo Filler Pen Company in Hamburg and their first pen, Rouge Et Noir, named after the Stendhal novel and made of black ebonite and with a red cap, was launched in 1909. It was, as the advertisement of the time put it, 'a fountain pen that does not make blots'. The Montblanc, introduced in the following year, was sold on the ground-breaking premise that it would not leak when closed.

By this time the fountain-pen industry was writing history with its new ideas: Sheaffer's lever-filler device of 1912, Parker's button-filler version… But the trio had stumbled on marketing gold. The Meisterstück's forerunner was so successful, and its branding was so memorable, that the company was renamed Montblanc Simplo. During the global depression of the 1930s it introduced a lifetime guarantee for the Meisterstück to drive home its quality message.

After the 1950s, as ballpoint technology improved, fountain pens became less popular as everyday writing tools, and the status they symbolized was in many ways more important than their utility. A Meisterstück protruding from a man's top pocket makes a statement about him – before anything is written.

Schreiben Sie
Ihre Grüße vom Strand mit
dem Montblanc Füllhalter

MONTBLANC
FÜLLHALTER

Top: President John F. Kennedy hands a Meisterstück back to Konrad Adenauer, the first chancellor of the Federal Republic of Germany, at a treaty signing in 1962. The Germans had been the first to prototype a fountain pen: in 1636, inventor Daniel Schwenter proposed using one quill inside another, then sealing it with cork. But it was not until Montblanc that iridium-tipped nibs, rubber that did not become brittle over time and ink that did not clog made the fountain pen a reality. **Above and left:** Montblanc's early advertising reflected the spirit and style of the times and in some cases the company had the confidence not to show its pens at all.

AVIATOR SUNGLASSES

ACCESSORIES

A menswear icon is a staple of the male wardrobe that has held this position over generations, but Hollywood can certainly be helpful in winning it this accolade. Perhaps no accessory has been reborn with more impact thanks to an appearance in a movie than Ray-Ban Aviators. In 1986's *Top Gun* student fighter pilots played by Tom Cruise and Val Kilmer competed to be best in their class. Their clothes may have provided limited opportunities for imitation – they wore flying suits for much of the film – but their Aviator sunglasses sparked massive worldwide sales.

Aviators have appeared in other films before and since: James Stewart wore a similar style in *The Spirit of St Louis* (1956), about Charles Lindbergh's pioneering trans-Atlantic flight; Peter Fonda wore them in *Easy Rider* (1969); and they have made appearances in several later period pieces, among them *13 Days* (2000), *Almost Famous* (2000) and *Pearl Harbor* (2001). But it was the machismo of *Top Gun* – a perfect vehicle for the brash spirit of the 1980s – that made them not only a classic, but also what is reputed to be the world's best-selling style of sunglasses.

Fashion may have taken note of the style because of the movie, but the film's costume designers did so for its authenticity. It was worn by the cast of *Top Gun* precisely because it was what fighter pilots wore, and still wear. The style was launched in 1929 after General MacCready of the United States military commissioned a manufacturer to design eye protection for United States Air Force pilots that would offer a clear field of vision, and reduce glare from the sun – which was causing headaches – and the effects of ultraviolet and infrared radiation on flyers' eyes. The commission was effectively responsible for the Ray-Ban company being established. In 1935 the military designated the style it helped to create as the Type D-1; the first time Aviators went on sale to the public was in 1936, when Ray-Ban was formed.

The original model had a plastic frame, so that no metal touched the faces of the ground crew working in subzero conditions (although it was later replaced by a

Opposite: 'I feel the need, the need for speed!' Tom Cruise as Maverick in Tony Scott's *Top Gun* (1986), the movie that started a craze for Ray-Ban's Aviator style of sunglasses (below).

gold-coloured metal one) and an antiglare lens in a distinctive green colour. This lens was a characteristic, oversized, side-on teardrop shape, much like that of the goggles already in service. Because the lenses came low over the cheeks to protect the entire eye socket, they were said to leave pilots with a Ray-Ban tan. Nevertheless, the style was embraced by naval flyers especially, and even came to be a mark of distinction. US army and air force pilots typically preferred a smaller, squarer style by American Optical, which was introduced in 1958; the glasses could be easily removed or put on while a helmet was worn.

Given the intimate association between the aviator style and combat flying, it is ironic that fighter and bomber pilots rarely wore only sunglasses until well after the Second World War. Goggles, sometimes tinted, were worn until the introduction of helmets with drop-down visors during the 1950s, and the early sunglasses were designed to accommodate them. Indeed, the military specification often referred to sunglasses as a category of goggle. It was not until 1941 that D-1 goggles were officially replaced by what were at last referred to as 'Glasses, Flying, Sun, Rose Smoke, Type 2'.

Opposite: Robert de Niro as Travis Bickle in Martin Scorsese's *Taxi Driver* (1976). The sunglasses represented a barrier between Bickle's warped internal world and the outside reality in which he could barely exist. **Below:** Aviator-style sunglasses in the real world, worn by US Navy flyers and ship's personnel alike, here opting for the squarer American Optical style.

THE DIVING WATCH

ACCESSORIES

When Mercedes Gleitze became the first woman to swim the English Channel, in 1927, her success was marred when a hoaxer claimed to have done so in a shorter time. So, just a fortnight later, she set out to swim the 35 or so kilometres (22 miles) again in what was dubbed the Vindication Swim. It received considerable publicity and Hans Wilsdorf, founder of the Rolex watch company, realizing the marketing potential of sponsoring her, asked her to wear one of his new Oyster watches. Gleitze had to be pulled out of the water 11 kilometres (7 miles) short of the shore – but a journalist from *The Times* noted she was wearing a gold watch on a ribbon around her neck; it was still keeping perfect time. And a legend was born. One month later the Rolex Oyster Perpetual was launched in the United Kingdom.

Wilsdorf, a German watchmaker, had moved to London in 1906 and founded the Rolex brand in 1908; the name was said to emulate the sound of a mechanical watch being wound and worked internationally. The company was based in Geneva from 1912 to save on export duties. Wilsdorf, and his partner and brother-in-law Alfred Davis, had originally made cases and imported movements. However, with Cartier's creation, in 1904, of what is recognized as the first wristwatch – for the aviator Alberto Santos-Dumont – this style began to replace pocket watches and Wilsdorf saw his opportunity.

The Rolex Watch Company immediately set about creating a new breed of tough watches unassailable by the elements. In 1910 it received the first official chronometer certification for a wristwatch; and the creation of water-resistant watches continued to progress. But it was not until Rolex bought the rights to the patent for a screw-down crown from Swiss watchmaker Perret & Perregaux that the Oyster could finally be realized. In 1926 the first dustproof, airtight and, most impressively for the time, waterproof watch was launched.

Further advances included the addition of a self-winding movement in 1931. This meant the crown was only occasionally unscrewed to adjust the time, which saved wear on seals and enabled the watch to remain waterproof for longer. In 1945 a date display mechanism was created, leading to the Oyster Perpetual Datejust. The Rolex Submariner, the first watch to be waterproof to a depth of 100 metres (328 feet), came in 1953 and made the leap from specialist tool to luxury item. The Explorer was introduced in 1954, the GMT Master, the first dual-time watch, in 1955, the Sea Dweller in 1967 and the Cosmograph Daytona in 1976.

Other watches may be more striking than the basic Oyster, and even more accurate. But few have been more desired, as the counterfeiting industry's backhanded compliment suggests. It has come to define the archetypal watch: simple but sturdy, smart but manly. Thanks to a special service organized by Wilsdorf, British prisoners of war during the Second World War were able to order, by letter and direct from their camps, an Oyster – typically a Speed King. Corporal Clive Nutting, one of the organizers of the famous Great Escape, ordered an expensive 3525 chronograph and, although he was not an officer, was afforded the same arrangement. The watch was said to have been used to time sentry movements and so aid escape attempts. Wilsdorf took a serviceman's word as his bond and was happy to wait for payment when the war ended; this boosted morale as the arrangement implied the Axis forces would be defeated.

Tenzing Norgay and Edmund Hillary wore Oysters when they conquered Everest in 1953, and the watch worked well at some 8848 metres (29,000 feet) above sea level. Seven years later the special edition Sea Dweller, worn by pioneering diver Jacques Piccard, performed at the bottom of the Mariana Trench, at 10,916 metres (35,800 feet) the deepest point on earth. However, perhaps the greatest accolade is found in fiction: an Oyster Perpetual was James Bond's choice in Ian Fleming's novels, with a Submariner chosen by the Bond of the movie franchise until 1995.

Opposite top: The Rolex Submariner. **Opposite, bottom left:** The original Oyster watch. **Opposite, bottom right:** An early Oyster Christmas advertisement: 'Make it a Rolexmas'. The Oyster's waterproof properties were stressed in all early advertising. As one advertisement for the UK newspaper the *Daily Mail* had it, the watch 'can, in consequence, be worn in the sea or bath without injury, nor would arctic or tropical conditions affect the wonderful precision of its beautifully poised movement'. The Oyster's launch, it added, 'marks a unique development in the forwards stride of the chronomatic science'. **Below:** Mercedes Gleitze.

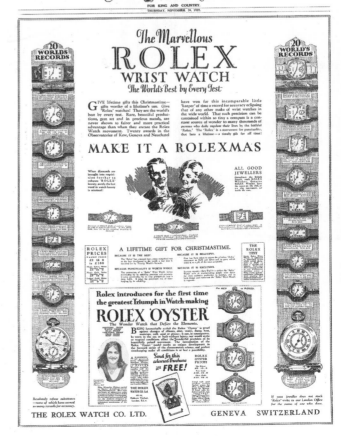

THE ALL-WEATHER LIGHTER

ACCESSORIES

The Zippo was not an entirely original idea. The story has it that in 1931 George Blaisdell, founder of the company of the same name, saw a friend at the Bradford Country Club in Pennsylvania struggling to use an Austrian-made lighter. On the plus side, its chimney design meant it was almost impossible for the flame to be blown out by the wind. On the downside, the oval case was flimsy and two hands were required to operate the lighter because the lid had to be fully removed.

Blaisdell knew a good idea when he saw one. He used the perforated chimney design – the heart of the Zippo's iconography – and created a tough, rectangular case with a hinged, sprung, flip-top lid. All told, there were some 22 components in brass, aluminium and steel, with a wick. In 1933 the first Zippo was launched. Blaisdell gave it this name because he liked the sound of the word zipper (then an innovation itself) for its sense of modernity. The lighter came with a lifetime guarantee ('It works or we'll fix it for free', as the packaging had, and still has, it). The patent for the design was filed the following year and granted in 1936. By 2006, some 425 million Zippo lighters had been sold.

Key advances, made by the 1950s, were stamping the case from single pieces of metal, which gave the lighter its distinctive rounded edges, and moving the lid spring mechanism from outside the case to inside it. This created a smooth outer shell that not only looked elegantly streamlined, but also saved many a man's trouser pocket. Otherwise the Zippo, like many iconic products, has barely changed. Even the endless variety of decals is an old idea; the lighter was first used as an advertising medium in the mid-1930s, when Bradford's Kendall Refining Company ordered 500 with its logo. In doing so it created a Holy Grail for avid collectors – for whom Zippo launched an international 'swap meet' in 1995. Major national events all over the world are invariably celebrated by a Zippo edition.

Other Zippo products have come and gone: a pocket knife, a flashlight, pens, pencils and even a lighter-shaped car. But only the lighter has stood the test of time. However, it was the Second World War that made it an American icon, even though it was not available to civilians. It was adopted as part of every GI's unofficial kit, and the military eventually commissioned its own version, which used a black paint to protect its cheaper steel case from rust (all brass was co-opted for the war effort). When it was baked, the paint gave what was called a crackle finish.

Later, the surface of the lighter proved to be a perfect site for customization and personal messages. 'If you want to make love, smile when you hand me back the lighter' was engraved on one that belonged to a smooth-talking serviceman in Vietnam. And the marketing benefits of wartime tales – that Zippos had deflected enemy bullets, or that servicemen lost at sea were spotted by rescuers when they lit theirs – did not go unnoticed by the company.

The Zippo's iconic status was enhanced when it became a prop for movie stars such as Ingrid Bergman in *Casablanca* (1942), as well as for rock 'n' rollers after the Second World War; the distinctive metallic click when it is opened has even been sampled for songs. Eric Clapton is said to have used this as a metronomic device when he was composing.

THE MOON WATCH

ACCESSORIES

Other watches have been worn in space: models by Breitling (its Cosmonaute was chosen for NASA's early orbital flights in 1962, and publicized with an advertisement that read 'Watch in Space!'), Omega – also for NASA – and Fortis, for the Russian Space Administration. Bell & Ross entered the market in 1992 with its Space 1, a re-edition of the first automatic chronograph worn in space in 1983 by the German astronaut Reinhart Furrer on SpaceLab. But only one watch can claim to be the first to be worn on the moon: the Omega Speedmaster.

NASA believed there was too little time before its first manned missions to the moon to commission a watch designed from scratch. So in 1962 it tested ten brands of chronograph anonymously purchased in Houston, Texas, and, after eliminating four, requested two models from each of the remaining six brands; the Speedmaster had already been worn in space, also in 1962, by the astronaut Walter Schirra, who bought it for himself. Omega won the official NASA account for technical reasons three years later – with a version of a watch launched in 1957, ten months before Sputnik, which had been designed with sport rather than space travel in mind .

The Swiss watchmaker had developed an acrylic glass that gave maximum visibility in all conditions and would not shatter into tiny pieces if broken – even a tiny piece of sharp glass, hurtling around in a spacecraft at several tens of thousands of miles an hour, can result in a catastrophic puncture. The Speedmaster was selected again in 1981 when the launch of the space shuttle prompted NASA to conduct an equipment review.

The Speedmaster was more than adornment. Wearing a watch, now as then, benefited astronauts psychologically by connecting them with the earth. And during the early years of the space race a watch was also genuinely functional. When there was a complete systems failure during the Apollo 13 mission of 1972, the astronauts used their Speedmasters to time the rocket burst that aligned their capsule for re-entry to the earth's atmosphere.

The watch was also water resistant to a depth of 60 metres (196 feet), an indication of the sturdiness of the screwed-back case, designed by Claude Baillod, which was able to withstand all space could throw at it: the need to operate in a vacuum and zero gravity, temperature extremes on the moon of -160°C (-255°F) to 120°C (248°F), and the huge G-forces of take-off and re-entry. With functional details including a highly legible dial and outsize crown and pushers, so that the chronograph might be operated while wearing heavy gloves, it was no surprise the Speedmaster passed NASA's rigorous testing, which surpassed anything that might be applied to a more earthbound watch.

Despite ongoing pressure for an American-made watch to be selected, astronauts Virgil Grissom and John Young used the first NASA-approved Speedmasters for 1965's Gemini Titan III mission, and Edward White wore it on the first American space walk two months later. Omega discovered that its watch had been worn only after seeing it in press photographs, and added 'Professional' to its dial in recognition of this fact.

In 1969 the Speedmaster became the first watch to be worn on the moon – not by Neil Armstrong, who left his inside the capsule as a back-up in case watches failed in the moon's atmosphere, but by Buzz Aldrin. Indeed, no other watch can claim, as one Speedmaster advertisement did, that it was, 'Tested in Switzerland. Tested in Houston. Tested on the Moon.'

Below: Omega was quick to make the most of the marketing potential when NASA selected its Speedmaster design as official astronauts' equipment.

This page: While it has remained largely true to its first incarnation, the Speedmaster has evolved over the years. Here, from top to bottom, are models from 1957 (the first, with its broad arrow hour-hand), 1966 and 1989 (marked Professional).

THE NECKTIE

ACCESSORIES

Opposite: The Duke of Windsor, later Edward VIII, wears his tie knot narrow to squeeze it into the narrow confines of his pin collar. His grandfather, Edward VII, is said to have inspired the wider, triangular, full or double Windsor knot – his ties were made with especially thick cloth to produce a wider knot even when they were tied into the traditional four-in-hand. The Windsor allowed those wearing more standard ties to carry a wider knot, in emulation. It has the benefit of not slipping away from the collar. Below: 1960s advertisements for ties – a Hardy Amies model strikes a pose with negatives in 1962, and a booklet for Gieves, the Savile Row tailor that acquired Hawkes & Co. in 1974 to form Gieves & Hawkes.

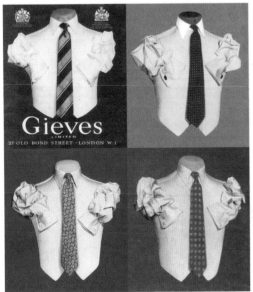

The tie's function is to decorate. It does not keep any part of the body warm, nor does it secure another garment in place. What it does do, is bring colour and pattern where it is often lacking – in men's formal attire. The modern tie dates only to 1924 when Jesse Langsdorf, an American tailor, patented an 'all-weather, wrinkle-free' design that is characteristic of most neckties in western dress today: three pieces of cloth, stitched and folded into a point and, most pertinently, with the fabric cut on the bias, at a 45-degree angle to the fibres of the material, so that the tie can be knotted and untied without being almost permanently creased.

Until the 1940s ties were comparatively short. The idea was to provide a flourish of colour at the neck, hence the emphasis on width (and extravagant pattern) rather than length. For a garment as simple as a tie, fashions have been extreme, from the minimalistic boot-lace variety that dates back to the 1860s to the wide kipper tie of the 1970s, created by Michael Fish – founder in 1966 of the influential Savile Row tailors Mr Fish.

Despite the tie's seeming frivolity, its origins are military. Roman legionaries on Trajan's Column in Rome, which dates from the second century AD, are shown wearing what is said to be the earliest recorded example of neckwear: a scarf-like *focale*. The soldiers of the terracotta army of Shih Huang Ti and the Qin dynasty (221–206 BC) wore silk cords around their necks, although more as a symbol of status than an article of clothing. But it was not until the sixteenth century that something akin to the modern, decorative tie appeared. During Europe's Thirty Years War (1618–48) Croatian mercenaries in the French army sported neckwear similar to a cravat (the word is a linguistic mangling of Croat), ostensibly to signal their comradeship. Louis XIV of France adopted the style and gave it credibility in civilian society.

During the early eighteenth century the cravat morphed into stocks – a strip of muslin wound repeatedly around the neck and then pinned into place. From the 1850s, this developed into the looser, simple four-in-hand, a knotted, rectangular piece of cloth that, in turn, elongated to become a more structured version that could be tied into a neat knot suitable for the new turn-down shirt collars of the turn of the twentieth century.

From the 1920s ties striped in regimental colours were widely worn by British armed forces personnel at functions that required civilian dress. In the United States the influential men's outfitters Brooks Brothers took the style and made it a menswear standard, with one change: while the stripes on regimental ties ran from the left shoulder down to the right, Brooks' version ran from the right down to the left. The rep tie, called after the weave of the silk used in its construction, soon became an Ivy League style fixture. Certain colour coordinations were especially popular: the Prince of Wales' Foot Guards tie, in blue and maroon, was a best-seller.

British universities had already popularized wearing striped ties to denote membership of their colleges: in 1880 students at Exeter College, Oxford, began donning the ribbons from their straw boaters as a form of neckwear. Ties in college colours soon followed. Similarly, gentlemen's private clubs adopted their own ties. Anecdotally at least, this tradition was prompted by a joke. The actor Norman Forbes-Robertson, a prominent member of London's esteemed, thespian Garrick Club, wore a pale-pink and green tie to lunch one day and, when he was asked about its origin, quipped that it was the official club tie. Soon after, it was adopted as such.

FURTHER READING

Hardy Amies, *The Englishman's Suit*, Quartet, London 1994

Cally Blackman, *One Hundred Years of Menswear*, Laurence King Publishing, London 2009

Martin Brayley and Richard Ingram, *The World War II Tommy: British Army Uniforms European Theatre, 1939-45*, Crowood Press, Marlborough, 2007

Charlotte Brunel, *The T-Shirt Book*, Assouline, New York 2002

Gisbert L. Brunner and Christian Pfeiffer-Belli, *Wristwatches*, Könemann, Cologne 2006

Alan D. Cirker, *The Alpha Story*, Baker Hill Publishing, Chantilly, VA 2009

Henri-Paul Enjames, *GI Collector's Guide*, volumes I and II, Histoire & Collections, Paris 2003

Mick Farren, *The Black Leather Jacket*, Plexus, London 2008

Mary Lisa Gavenas, *The Fairchild Encyclopedia of Menswear*, Fairchild Books, New York 2008

Dale Hope, *The Aloha Shirt: Spirit of the Islands*, Beyond Words Publishing, Oregon 2000

Nick Knight, *Skinhead*, Omnibus, London 1982

Oscar Lenius, *A Well-Dressed Gentleman's Pocket Guide*, Prion, London 1998

Bernhard Roetzel, *Gentleman: A Timeless Fashion*, Könemann, Cologne 2004

Josh Sims, *Cult Streetwear*, Laurence King Publishing, London 2010

Josh Sims, *Rock Fashion*, Omnibus, London 1999

C.G. Sweeting, *Combat Flying Clothing: Army Air Forces Clothing during World War II*, Smithsonian Institution Press, Washington, D.C. 1984

László Vass and Magda Molnár, *Handmade Shoes for Men*, Könemann, Cologne 2008

Richard Windrow and Tim Hawkins, *The World War II GI: US Army Uniforms, 1941-45*, Crowood Press, Marlborough 2008

INDEX

PICTURE CREDITS

p.103b Courtesy Jockey

p.104 © Bettmann/Corbis

p.105 © Sunset Boulevard/Corbis

p.106 Courtesy Hanes

pp.107-8 Courtesy Fruit of the Loom

p.109 Michael Rougier/Time Life Pictures/Getty Images

p.110 Courtesy Gieves & Hawkes

p.111 Courtesy of the Advertising Archives

p.112 Photo by John Kobal Foundation/Getty Images

p.114 Photo by George Hurrell/John Kobal Foundation/Getty Images

p.115l Courtesy Huntsman

p.115r Courtesy Hardy Amies Archive

p.116 Courtesy Anderson and Sheppard

p.117 Courtesy Hardy Amies Archive

p.118 © Bettmann/Corbis

p.119tl Courtesy Hardy Amies Archive

p.119bl Teresa McWilliams for Hardy Amies archive

p.119r Courtesy Gieves & Hawkes

p.120l Courtesy Gieves & Hawkes

p.120r Courtesy Huntsman

p.121 Copyright owned by Arcadia Group Ltd (formerly called Montague Burton Ltd), 1939

p.122 Courtesy Brooks Brothers

p.123 Photo by Michael Rougier/Time Life Pictures/Getty Images

p.124 © Bettmann/Corbis

p.125 Courtesy Gieves & Hawkes

p.126 Courtesy of the Advertising Archives

pp.127-9 Copyright owned by Arcadia Group Ltd (formerly called Montague Burton Ltd), 1939

p.130t Courtesy Gieves & Hawkes

p.130b Courtesy Anderson and Sheppard

p.131 Photo by Silver Screen Collection/Hulton Archive/Getty Images

p.132 The Kobal Collection

p.134 Photo by Robert Whitaker/Getty Images

p.135 Courtesy Gieves & Hawkes

p.136 Courtesy Thomas Pink

p.137 Courtesy Brooks Brothers

p.138 © John Springer Collection/Corbis

p.139 © Bettmann/Corbis

p.140 The Print Collector/HIP/Topfoto

p.141 MGM/The Kobal Collection

p.142 Courtesy Brooks Brothers

p.143 © Bettmann/Corbis

p.144tl Courtesy Flamborough Manor

p.144tr Courtesy Flamborough Manor

p.144bl Courtesy Le Tricoteur

p.144br Courtesy Flamborough Manor

p.145 Courtesy Le Tricoteur

p.146 © 1956–2009 Tori Richard, Ltd. All rights reserved. Copyright rights protected under the Berne Convention throughout the World. Any unauthorized copying, distribution or adaptation (including of the designs depicted) is strictly prohibited, and may result in liability of up to $150,000.00 plus attorneys' fees and costs in the United States, and substantial liabilities under the laws of the country in which any infringement takes place.

p.147 CBS-TV/The Kobal Collection

pp.148-9 © 1956-2009 Tori Richard, Ltd. All rights reserved. Copyright rights protected under the Berne Convention throughout the World. Any unauthorized copying, distribution or adaptation (including of the designs depicted) is strictly prohibited, and may result in liability of up to $150,000.00 plus attorneys' fees and costs in the United States, and substantial liabilities under the laws of the country in which any infringement takes place.

pp.150-1 Courtesy Lacoste

p.152 Courtesy Fred Perry

p.153l Courtesy Lacoste

p.153r Courtesy Fred Perry

p.154 Photo by Popperfoto/Getty Images

pp.155-7 Courtesy Pendleton Woolen Mills

p.158 Courtesy Amor Lux

p.159 Photo by Michael Ochs Archive/Getty Images

p.160 Photo by Hulton Archive/Getty Images

p.161 Everett Collection/Rex Features

p.162 Photo by Hulton Archive/Getty Images

pp.164-5 Courtesy Dunhill

p.166 Courtesy Lock & Co/www.lockhatters.co.uk

p.167 Photo by Anwar Hussein/Hulton Archive/Getty Images

pp.168-9 Courtesy Brent Black

pp.170-1 Courtesy Montblanc

p.172 Paramount/The Kobal Collection

p.173 Ray-Ban/Luxottica

p.174 Courtesy Randolph Engineering Inc.

pp.176-7 Courtesy Rolex

pp.178-9 Courtesy Zippo

pp.180-1 Courtesy Omega

p.182t Courtesy Hardy Amies Archive

p.182b Courtesy Gieves & Hawkes

p.183 Photo by Hirz/Getty Images-